wall hangings

Embroidery by children of Andean Village, Peru. Courtesy, Gordon J. Cloney II, President, The Andean Foundation.

wall hangings:

designing with fabric and thread

sarita r. rainey

supervisor of art, *montclair, new jersey public schools*

author, *weaving without a loom*

davis publications, inc.
worcester, massachusetts

Copyright 1971
Davis Publications, Inc.
Worcester, Massachusetts, U.S.A.

Library of Congress Catalog Card Number:
70-142423
SBN: 87192-035-2

Printing: Davis Press, Inc.

Type: Univers

Design: Panagiota Darras

Front cover: *Tapestry. Student, Grade 7.*

Back cover: *Hawaiian quilted banners.* Artist,
the author.

All photographs by the author unless otherwise
credited.

Appliqué in navy blue and white.

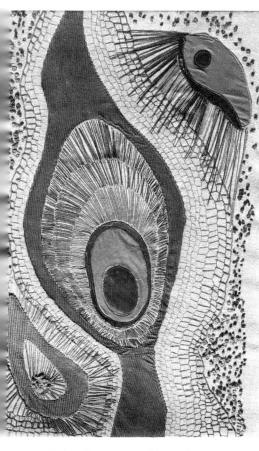

...th: symbolic of seeds, machine stitched ...roy and velvet, detached buttonhole stitch ...s net.

contents

foreword   6

introduction   7

learning to see   14

approaches to design   18

appliqué hangings   27

   Appliqué Hangings
   Reverse Appliqué Hangings
   Three-Dimensional Appliqué Hangings
   Fringed Appliqué Hangings

stitchery hangings   48

   Designing Wall Hangings with Threads and
     Stitches
   Hangings in Black and White Thread
   Hangings in Crewel Wool
   Canvas Stitched Hangings
   Hangings in Machine Stitchery
   Quilted Hangings

decorative treatments   92

varieties of approaches   99

   Mini-hangings

yarn painting   107

innovative combinations   108

   Collage Hangings
   Assemblage Hangings
   Banners
   Optical Hangings
   Other Combinations
   Woven and Knotted Threads

finishing a hanging   134

artists at work   142

appendix   150

glossary   154

bibliography   155

color section following page 104

   Colorful hangings by students

foreword

There has been a tendency for our society to believe that personal expression can take place only in the areas of painting and sculpture. This unfortunately has kept many people from enjoying broad experiences with other materials and processes. Our school programs, in the past, emphasized experiences in drawing and painting, forgetting the easy identification people have with the areas of the crafts.

The experiences of Sarita Rainey as an art educator and artist make it possible for her to effectively present *Wall Hangings: Designing with Fabric and Thread* to the reader. She removes the mystique surrounding the process of creating and makes it possible for students at any level of achievement to enjoy working with fabrics. In addition to learning how to use the materials, Miss Rainey helps her readers in developing understanding of design.

In *Wall Hangings: Designing with Fabric and Thread* Miss Rainey is helping to fill the need for information about the crafts and, particularly, the crafts in education. She has provided an opportunity for teachers, students and practicing craftsmen to broaden their areas of art experiences.

Donald L. Wyckoff

Machine stitchery. Artist, Merry Bean.

Mr. Donald L. Wyckoff is Executive Vice President and National Director of the American Crafts Council.

Each of us has an urge, consciously or otherwise, to make a personal statement through some medium of art expression. Making a fabric and thread wall hanging offers an exciting and creative outlet for this urge—a challenging, imaginative activity for any age level—and of special significance for the school art program.

Many of us, seeing a wall hanging for the first time, may miss the full meaning implied in the design, but we comprehend color, line, texture, and shape when presented in an organized arrangement. Once we make a wall hanging and have the experience of manipulating fabric and thread into a composition, we shall appreciate more fully the creative use of materials and the uniqueness of an idea visually presented.

If artists are asked why they create, the reasons will usually be as numerous as those to whom the question is directed. Fabric and thread bring the designer close to his true world—a world of color and texture that he can arrange and rearrange until arriving at an organized pattern. For some, this is a way of making historical techniques live again in a modern environment. Still others may think of fabric and thread as materials that encourage the designer to discriminate as he selects, especially with combinations of similar

introduction

Moon Man: quilted appliqué.

Embroidery by children of Andean Village, Peru. Courtesy, Gordon J. Cloney II, President, The Andean Foundation.

and dissimilar materials such as those native to his environment.

This book attempts to show how different artists (children and adults) speak and how the reader can discover and portray personal impressions with imaginative wall hangings designed in colorful thread and fabric. As a source of inspiration, numerous close-up and full view examples of student and professional work are presented—the latter to familiarize the reader and his students with wall hanging techniques and materials common to the contemporary artist. For those who wish detailed information about procedures, techniques are provided to illustrate a variety of approaches. Whether student or teacher, novice or skilled designer, amateur or professional artist, this book offers ideas and techniques for creating fabric hangings in appliqué and stitchery. Emphasis is on design and its application. No one method is advocated, but rather, the material is presented as suggestions for getting started in this fascinating and imaginative art form.

Circus train: felt and cotton prints on burlap background, accented with rickrack and metallic edging. Grade 1.

South Bank: colorful fabrics arranged in a pattern. Artist, Mary Pilcher, England.

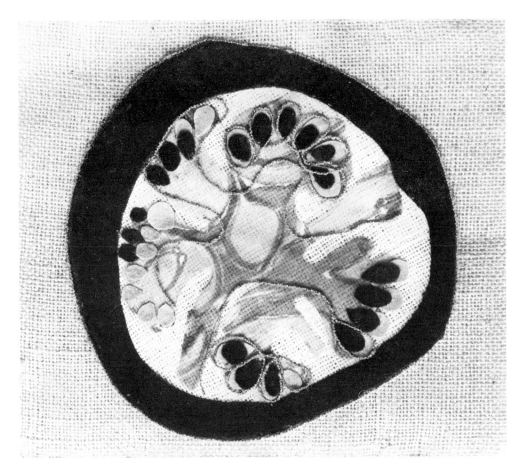

Internal structure of fruit: chiffon center accented with felt. Student, Grade 5.

Flowers: yarn stitchery on a burlap background. Student, Grade 3.

The Visitation: stitchery. Artist, Sister Mary Helena Steffens-Meier, O.S.F. Courtesy, American Crafts Council.

Below, left to right—
People. Student, Grade 1. Milwaukee, Wisconsin. Kent Anderson, Art Supervisor.
Boy: woolen and cotton cloth edged in yarn stitching. Student, Grade 2.
Girl: cotton print edged in yarn. Student, Grade 2.
Clown: yarn on burlap. Student, Grade 4.

The Clowns: stitchery. Artist, Martha Miller. Courtesy, Contemporary Crafts Museum.

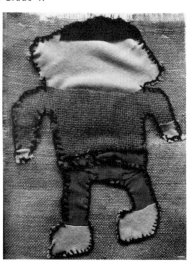

Freedom's Door: appliqué and stitchery based on idea of Berlin Wall, barbed wire, and door to escape. Artist, Nancy Yost.

And He took us forth from Egypt: calligraphy. Artist, Lillian Elliott. Courtesy, American Crafts Council.

Medieval Arabian map of the world. Artist, Elspeth Hart.

Border: canvas, with design in colored wool. Russian 19th century. The Metropolitan Museum of Art, Rogers Fund, 1909.

Fragment of white linen with Arabic inscription embroidered in silver gilt thread. The Metropolitan Museum of Art. Gift of George D. Pratt, 1931.

Detail of panel: white satin embroidered in polychrome silks and purl. English XVII C. The Metropolitan Museum of Art, Rogers Fund, 1908.

History

Considered by many to be a contemporary art form, appliqué and stitchery actually date back to primitive man when he first laced furs and hides together to make clothing and decorative designs. As man became more skillful, he stitched designs on cloth to enhance its appearance, using the color and texture of the stitches to embellish clothing, temple hangings and ceremonial vestments. Even replicas of tapestries woven during the Middle Ages originated in what was then called embroidery.

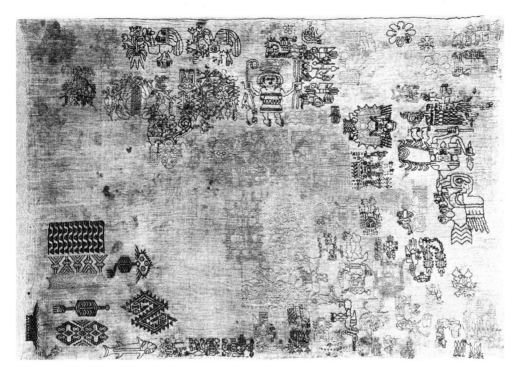

Down through the years the term embroidery has been used to include different kinds of needlework: petit (small) and gros (large) point stitches, as well as appliqué (the art of attaching fabric, hide, sticks, bone, and the like to a background) as ways of creating designs. Contemporary embroidery, however, is often referred to as stitchery, a broader term implying more latitude—more imaginative use of materials. Hand in hand with the development of man, we find that stitchery has flourished as a functional and decorative art. And today, it continues to inspire rediscovery of the past and relates its charm—and challenge—to personal expression in the world of today.

Sampler 27¾'' x 41¼''. Peru: Nazca c. 200 B.C. The Museum of Primitive Art, New York.

Llama and cow embroideries by children of Chijnaya. Exhibition circulated by the Smithsonian Museum.

Embroideries by children of Chijnaya. Exhibition circulated by the Smithsonian Museum.

Photo, courtesy Patricia Trotter.

Photo, courtesy Patricia Trotter.

As we look around with an inquiring eye, we see almost limitless sources of inspiration for design: the outlines of leaf or flower forms, the grouping of grassy clumps, the pattern of branches against the sky, snow-covered trees, the arrangement of shells and rocks on a beach, the texture and pattern of wood. In addition, imagine looking at the world through a magnifying glass or microscope: the busy city traffic, the pattern of overlapping buildings, the cluster of umbrellas against a beach, towering structures against the sky. This is our real world. There is also the world of fantasy—a world of make-believe—one that will stir the imagination. What is it like to live in the jungle or desert, to be a man on Mars or to fly to Venus?

Collecting, sketching and photographing are basic ways to record things we see, think, and feel for future study. Collections provide firsthand information about textures and design. Sketches or photographs reflect the general pattern of objects: a lamp post, building front, utensil, insect, fruit, or animal shape; or emphasize parts of things: the wing of a bird, the hoof of a cow, the form of a tail, the veins of a leaf, or the shape of a nose.

We should interpret our visual recordings in our own way, and personalize our methods of stating the same subject—be it a way to combine color, texture, and space, or to interpret an everyday scene.

Many everyday items, common to our environment, suggest ideas that inspire both the student and professional designer:

• A wheel form suggests radiating lines and circles.

• Rocks appear as overlapping shapes, offering endless ideas for variety in pattern.

learning to see

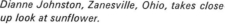
Dianne Johnston, Zanesville, Ohio, takes close-up look at sunflower.

- Boards, interspersed with knots and lines, suggest ideas for textural thread drawings.

- Plant leaves offer ideas for experimental thread design.

- Thistles suggest detail and shape for textural drawings in stitchery.

- Milkweed pods suggest interesting forms.

- Pine cones provide ideas for texture and form.

- Seaweed suggests ideas for overlapping stitches.

- Fabrics and yarns suggest pattern.

We must learn to see, select and analyze before translating what we see into visual images. Our perception is expanded by close-up looks at elements within our environment. Such views, translated into thread and fabric constructions, become individual responses, varying with each of us, to personalize our work.

A look at the inside of fruit. Student, Grade 5.

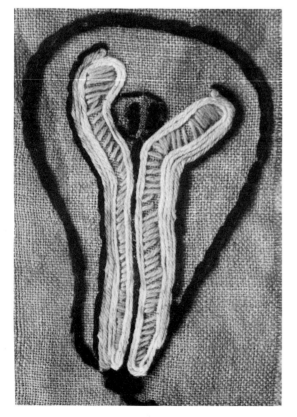

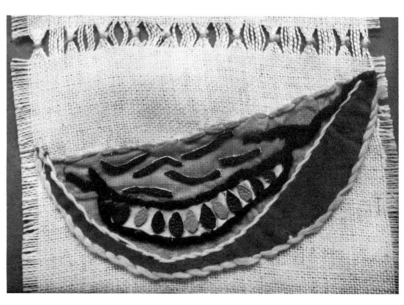

Thistle.

Interpreting an insect.   Student, Grade 5.

Interpreting animals.

Interpreting a bird.

Milkweed pod.

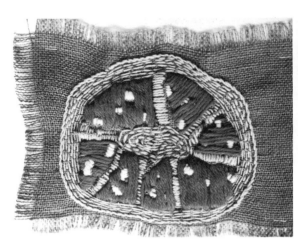

Stitched hanging of interior of fruit. Student, Grade 4.

Detail of a wall hanging design. Artist, Priscilla Sage.

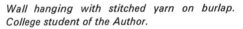

Wall hanging with stitched yarn on burlap. College student of the Author.

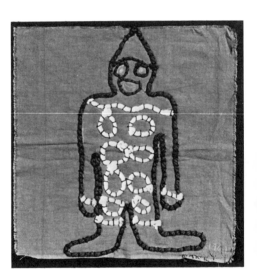

Student, Grade 2. Milwaukee, Wisconsin. Kent Anderson, Art Supervisor.

A fabric design is composed of elements used in different ways to express an idea. These elements: line, texture, form, space, color, and rhythm—are the skeletal parts of the composition.

approaches to design in fabric and thread

Line gives detail to shape, outlines a shape, creates texture by combining different kinds and lengths of line in an elaborate pattern of stitches, establishes direction and movement.

Texture is a pattern of different overlapping stitches that vary in size. It is rough, smooth, soft, or hard.

Form is a cutout shape, a solid mass of stitches, or an area enclosed by an outline.

Artist, Nancy Belfer.

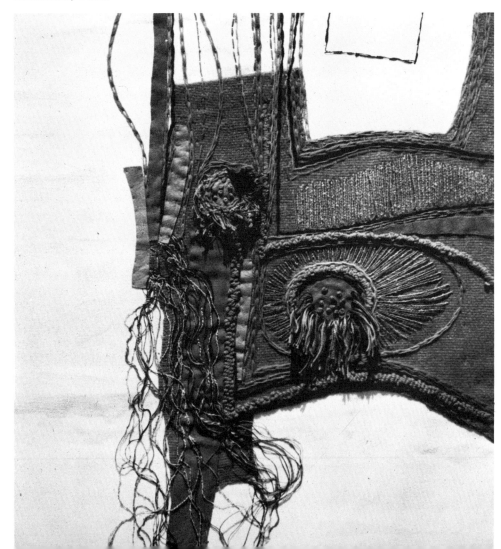

Space is an equal or unequal pattern (depending upon the design requirement) or the area around the form.

Color is subdued (the design and background the same or closely related in color), or strong contrast (the design and background of contrasting colors).

Rhythm is a repeat of any element: shape, line, form.

Artist, the author.

Student, Grade 3.

Student, Grade 5.

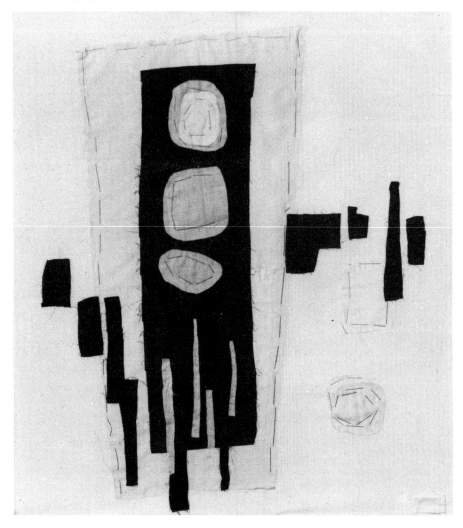

Try developing ideas with different techniques and media of your choice—drawing, painting, torn paper, crayon, and the like—then translate into fabric and thread hangings.

Suggested ways to develop a preliminary idea:

Drawing

• Use a crayon or felt tip marker and draw lines or forms that represent stitches.

• Experiment with different ways of outlining shapes.

• Develop a variety of flower shapes, then overlap them in various ways to form an allover pattern.

Crayon lines to represent stitches.

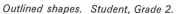

Outlined shapes. Student, Grade 2.

Overlapped flower shapes.

Student, Grade 2.

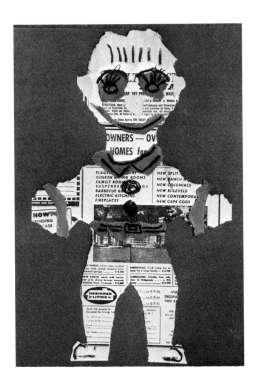

Torn and cut paper

- Interpret a rhythm beat in paper.

- Make animal shapes in paper.

- Make a torn-paper design and accent it with crayon.

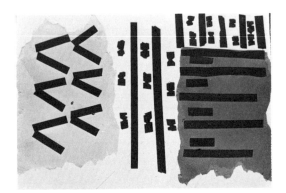

Student, Grade 4.

Student, Grade 4.

Crayon

- Make different width crayon lines.

- Make a crayon design and paint over it with tempera paint (crayon resist).

- Create a crayon picture.

- Scratch through a layer of crayon (crayon sgraffito).

Student, Grade 2.

Student, Grade 5.

Student, Grade 5.

Finger painting accented with crayon. Student, Grade 4.

Painting

• Make a finger painting and accent the unpainted areas with different colors of crayon.

• Make a design in paint with large forms.

• Finger paint over a crayon design.

Printmaking

• Cut a pattern or motif in linoleum, polystyrene, potato, or other such materials from which to print a design on fabric.

• Make a rubbing over a rough surface using tree bark, wood, or a cut paper design.

Finger paint over top of a crayon design. Student, Grade 2.

Make a potato print organizing the shapes in different patterns. Student, Grade 4.

Cord on a burlap background. Student, Grade 6.

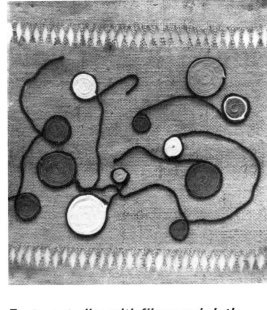

Texture studies with fibers and cloth

• Make different textural patterns with cord on a fabric background.

• Combine techniques such as rug hooking and stitchery to make texture.

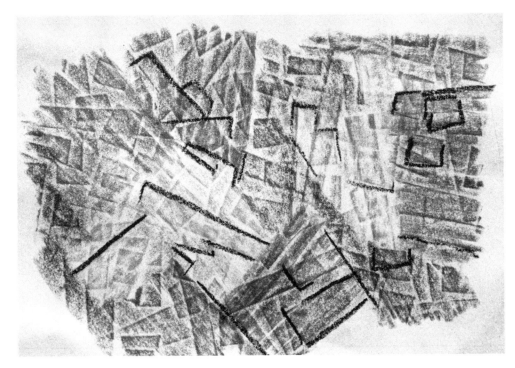

Create patterns by making a rubbing: place paper over a textural surface such as cut paper, screen or wood surface. Accent parts of the design to define the forms. Student, Grade 6.

Thread and paint. Artist, Dorothy Davis.

Crayon and yarn. Student, Grade 6.

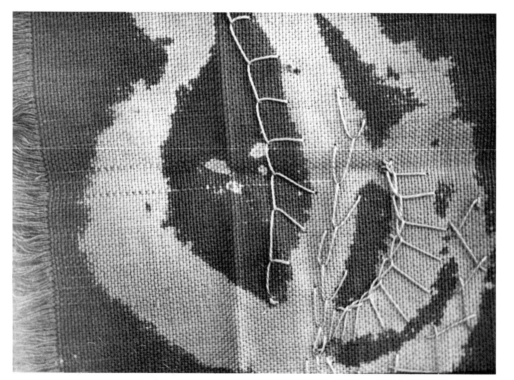

Bleached fabric and thread. Artist, Dorothy Davis.

Combine different materials

• Thread and paint: Accent a stitchery pattern with paint.

• Bleach and thread: Use bleach to remove a color; accent the resulting pattern with stitchery.

• Crayon and thread: Draw with crayon on fabric and accent it with stitchery.

Tie and dye a background fabric; develop a design in stitchery or appliqué related to the background.

People of any age can experience the pleasure of working directly with fabrics by seeing, feeling and handling various kinds of material. An appliqué hanging is an exciting way to portray the ideas resulting from these experiences.

Over the years, appliqué has evolved from a precisely planned, finely stitched pattern, to a lively relaxed form with ragged edges and fringed or decorative bindings. New and contemporary materials offer direction and challenge, but scraps left from sewing, or remnants purchased from a yard goods store should also be prominent on a list of materials.

Appliqué is the technique of pasting or stitching cut shapes or pieces of one material on top of another.

Reverse appliqué differs in procedure from basic appliqué in that one material having cut out areas is placed over a background material, exposing color of that material.

Relief or three-dimensional appliqué may protrude from a flat background or be suspended as a mobile form. Either technique may incorporate parts, pieces or entire shapes of non-fabric objects.

appliqué hangings

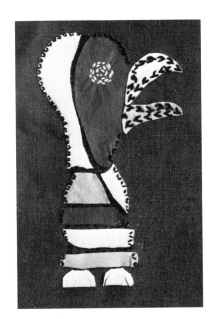

Appliqué. Student, Grade 6.

Reverse appliqué: Mola design. Collection, Mr. & Mrs. William B. Jennison.

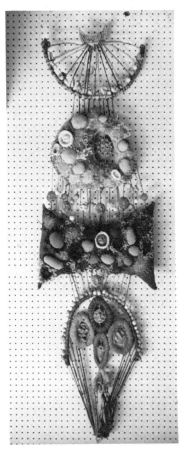

Stuffed cloth forms accented with unglazed clay. Artist, Priscilla Sage.

27

Amy Girdler, Old Greenwich, Conn.

Student, Grade 6.

Student, Grade 3.

Appliqué hangings

Appliqué includes the techniques of pasting, mono-rubbing, and stitching. Most appliqué hangings are made in two-dimensional design and are easily understood and appreciated by any age level. The designer may sensitively combine threads, floss, yarn, and fabric into lively compositions — personalized compositions that vibrate with color and rhythm. He may find a challenge by working with a diversity of materials and perhaps discover aesthetic relationships of shape, color, line, and texture—the ingredients for an exciting design.

Student, Grade 2. Milwaukee, Wisconsin. Kent Anderson, Art Supervisor.

28   appliqué hangings

Pasted appliqué technique

Pasted appliqué is the simplest form of two-dimensional appliqué.

Materials:
fabric
scissors
paste
yarn
thread
straight pins
needles
frame (optional)

Procedure

One might approach making a pasted appliqué hanging as he would a drawing, by first creating the major parts of the design. To begin, cut out large cloth shapes to represent the basic idea, then use smaller pieces to add detail and clarity to the design. Work fast. Stand away from the work; look at it from a distance to get a different perspective. Evaluate the composition: Does it fill the background area? Is the subject matter clearly defined? Are the colors repeated?

A pre-planned design is a helpful guide to determine the amount of fabric and size of the shape. Draw the design on paper or cloth. Arrange the design on background material and paste.

If the design is composed of several shapes, experiment with different arrangements (overlapping some pieces or varying the size of others) before pasting. Paste only the edges of each piece.

Design drawn with chalk on fabric.

Fabric piece cut out and pasted on burlap.

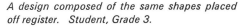
A design composed of the same shapes placed off register. Student, Grade 3.

Sean Taylor Murphy, Montclair, N. J.

Mono-rubbing is another direct technique for making fabric relief hangings.

Materials:

    spray cement (3-M), or spray starch
    scissors
    thread
    yarn
    fabric
    paper (any kind, including newspaper)

Mono-rub has design possibilities for both the beginner and professional. The process is similar to the finger paint mono-print method (mono meaning one) which is: First, make a finger painting design. Then, transfer the design while wet to the backing material by placing paper or cloth over the design and rubbing with the hand.

Appliqué mono-rub is a similar process except string, fabric, net, buttons, thread and yarn are used in lieu of paint. Almost any arrangement of these materials will make an effective design, and the process encourages spontaneity within the ability of all age levels. (See "Approaches to Design.")

If you wish to begin with a simple process and are willing to try new material arrangements and space relationships, appliqué mono-print offers new directions for explorations. As you readily can see, it is a rapid way to design a hanging.

To get started:

• Prepare a flat working surface of cardboard, drawing paper, newsprint, or newspaper.

• Collect bits of string, threads, and fabrics and arrange on the working surface until you make a pleasing composition. (Look for ways to fill parts of the design and ways to leave parts open.)

• After the design is arranged, spray it with a 3-M cement.

• Lay a fabric (this will be the background) over the sprayed design and rub it by hand or use a paint roller to make the design items adhere to the cloth.

• Lift the fabric design by carefully pulling the working surface of paper away from the wall hanging.

Felt design outlined with rug yarn. College student, Marlis Spauschus.

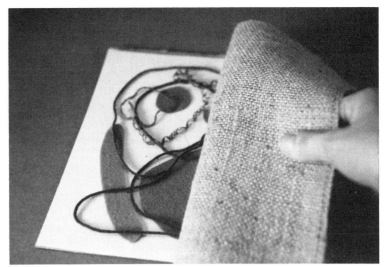
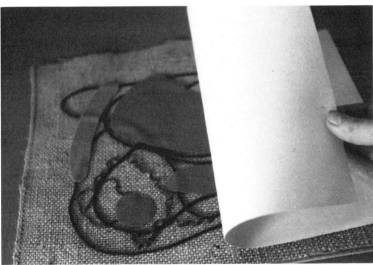
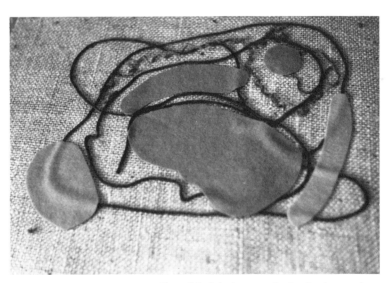

Completed design on a burlap background.

Variations

This simple wall hanging technique has many variations. Try different combinations of materials such as:

• net or pulled thread with string

• different weights of yarn

• metallic threads and cords

• chenille and pipe cleaners

• appliqué, burlaps, velvets, satins, with accents of buttons or sequins

• jute on different backgrounds

Experiment with different textures:

• knotted cords

• crossed threads

• interlaced strings

• frayed cords

• materials from nature—seeds, twigs, and feathers

Roving yarn or rug filler on a burlap background. Student, Grade 1.

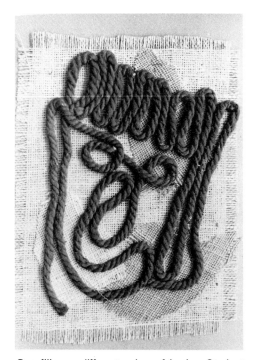

Rug filler on different colors of burlap. Student, Grade·5.

Felt and burlap used to create a mono-rub design on a background of felt. College student, Marlis Spauschus.

Frayed pieces of burlap and ravelings on burlap. Student, Grade 8.

Macramé cord and felt on burlap. Student, Grade 5.

Felt and string. Student, Grade 2.

An outline of rug filler on a crayon cloth background. Student, Grade 4.

Hand-stitched appliqué is a third technique that decorates and holds fabric in a permanent position, eliminating pasting and spraying.

The hand-stitched appliqué of the past was often precise and exact. Many stitches were made in only one size and confined to edges and borders. Contemporary stitching may also decorate edges. In addition, it meanders over and around the appliqué, encloses and creates form, and accents or fills space. It also may define a design or unify the background with the shape. Some stitches are innovative creations of the designer others are variations of traditional buttonhole, ladder, or chain stitches. These stitches may be combined into a single appliqué design, making a linear and textural pattern. Also, at times, the stitches may be used to hem the design shapes.

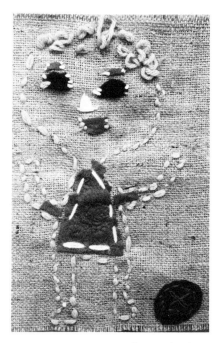

Stitchery encloses and creates form. Student, Grade 2.

Stitchery accents and fills space. Student, Grade 4.

Student, Grade 1.

Quiet Words. Artist, Lillian Elliott.

Quarry # 2. Artist, Gary Barlow.

Procedure

The technique of stitched appliqué can be treated as a sketch. Instead of using pencil, "sketch" the idea with fabric. Cut pieces of cloth into basic shapes and arrange them on a background, forming a composition. Add stitchery to clarify and emphasize the design.

Consider other design approaches, using fabric and thread for a collage, a painting, or composition. Incorporate non-fabric items of buttons, plastics, metallics, bells, and thread substitutes—raffia and straw. Use yarn and cloth instead of paint for splashes of color, and design with cutwork, silhouette shapes, and overlapping shapes.

Use yarn to outline a shape and secure in place with a couching or overcast stitch. Student, Grade 2.

Variations

Try some of the following design experiments:

• Combine sections of interwoven threads with embroidery. Overlap some parts and superimpose net over others.

• Compose a study of color tones in a single pattern (black, white, gray). Explore the combinations of burlaps and different weight yarn or synthetic and wool fabric with silk and wool thread.

• Experiment with closely related thread and fabric color combinations (red fabrics with wine, hot pink, etc.).

• Combine the techniques of appliqué, stitchery and rug hooking.

• Design a pattern with gauze and thread. Cut shapes from gauze (cheesecloth or other mesh cloth) and mount on a background of cotton or felt. Stitch around the edge of shapes for accent; weave threads of different weight through the gauze for added texture.

• Cut shapes and stitch their edges to a background; add embroidery on top of the shapes for accent.

Student, Grade 1.

Reverse appliqué mola made by Cuna Indians.
Collection of Mr. & Mrs. William B. Jennison.

Reverse appliqué hangings

Reverse or eyelet appliqué is, as the name implies, a reverse of appliqué—a fabric of cutout openings placed over a contrasting background to expose the color. By using multi-layers of fabric (each layer cut out exposing more underlying colors), one can create quite intricate designs.

Down through the centuries people of many cultures have varied the method of appliqué. The Cuna Indians of the San Blas Islands located off the Atlantic coast of Panama are known for using the reverse technique. Their molas (two panels stitched together to make a blouse) sparkle with imaginative motifs, ranging from symbolic tobacco plants to abstract maze patterns. This multi-layered, carved-like technique suggests still another way to make a decorative wall hanging design.

Materials:
  cloth—two, three, four pieces, each a
    different color
  paste, glue or needle and thread
  scissors

The edges of the cutout fabric areas are either hemmed or left raw. For hemming, use a soft cotton cloth pliable enough to lie flat when the edges are turned under. For raw edges, use a non-woven material that will not fray, such as soft felt. Felt is available in rich, vibrant colors making it particularly suitable for reverse appliqué, a technique that visually creates a pattern of color relationships. Poorly coordinated, young children will find felt is easy to cut and those with short attention spans can easily manipulate it.

Detail of mola design showing layers of fabric with hemmed edges. Collection of Mr. & Mrs. William B. Jennison.

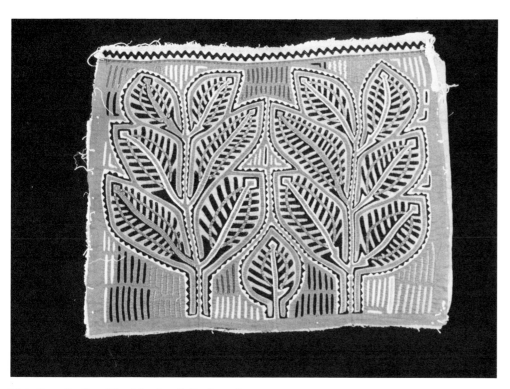

Mola from the San Blas Islands. Collection of
F. Louis Hoover.

*Reverse appliqué in layers of felt. Student
Grade 5.*

Layers of felt. Grade 5.

Felt. Grade 4.

For a variety of shades and tints, other than those found in felt or cottons of solid color, try dying fabric to make original color relationships. To make the dye spread evenly in tone, use desized cotton or remove the sizing by washing the pre-dyed fabric in soapy, lukewarm water.

Procedure

A good way to begin a reverse appliqué hanging is by making a color plan. Two successful methods for preparing this plan are to cut paper shapes or to crayon or paint cartoons.

For the first method, place several layers of construction paper together. Then cut out areas of each layer to expose the underlying layer.

For the second method, outline a shape and use crayon or paint to indicate the exposed fabric.

Once the design is made, there are several ways to transfer it to the fabric: Draw directly on the fabric, referring to the cut paper design; cut out a paper shape and trace around it; make a design on tracing paper and transfer it by using carbon paper with pencil or tracing wheel. Hold the layers together by gluing or stapling the outer edges of the fabric pieces. Following the color plan of the first or second method, cut out corresponding color for each layer of fabric, beginning with the top piece.

Allow extra material for the hem. Turn under edges around the openings, snipping corners and curves to make them lie flat. Stitch through all layers to hold the design securely in place. Use different kinds of stitches to decorate, or the blind stitch to conceal the edges.

Variations

The reverse appliqué illustrated shows the design results from cutting each fabric layer from top to bottom, but several other techniques are possible:

• Cut through two or three layers at one time to expose the bottom color.

• Put patches of different colors under the holes.

• Appliqué your choice of colors to the background of the top fabric layer.

• Stitch around or inside the cutout areas.

• Superimpose a block print on the top fabric or inside the openings of the underlying fabric.

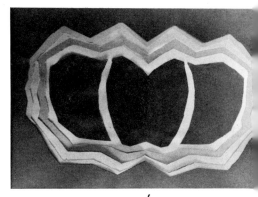

Shapes using reverse appliqué. Student, Grade 3.

Cut out areas of one color to expose the underlying colors.

Construction paper of different colors laid over one another.

Cut-out areas from a fabric.

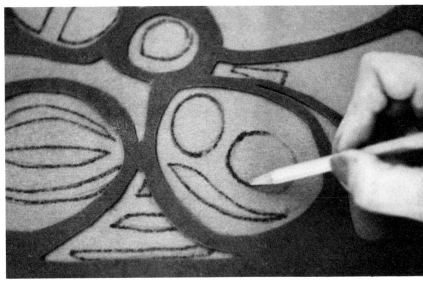

Place the cut-out design over another material. With a pencil, indicate the areas to be cut out from the second fabric.

Continue first two steps for as many layers as are needed to complete the design.

Three-dimensional construction made of tag board covered with felt on a felt base. Student, Grade 3.

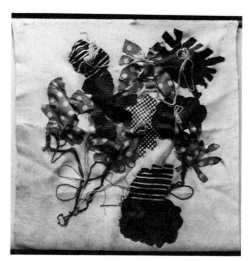

Stuffed appliqué shapes. Students, Educable.

Creature: a stuffed hanging. Artist, Jean A. Girdler.

Relief and three-dimensional hangings

Materials:
  fabric
  cotton stuffing (substitutes: nylon hosiery, scrap cloth, foam rubber)
  thread or yarn
  frameworks (wire, wood rods, reed, tree branches)
  scissors
  needles

A third kind of appliqué hanging includes bas-relief and sculptural form. Not all wall hangings need be flat. The third dimension can intrigue the imagination of children and older groups by focusing attention on protruding shapes (bas-relief), kinetic (moving) and suspended (equipoise) constructions.

The simplest three-dimensional (bas-relief) form is the padded or stuffed appliqué made with raised areas that protrude in varying amounts from the background surface.

Although there are many ways to make this type of appliqué hanging, two easy methods are as follows: The first and most common is to paste or stitch the edges of a shape to a background, leaving an opening to insert the stuffing. The second, less used method, is to make a stuffed shape by stitching the edges of two pieces of cloth of the same size together, leaving a small opening to insert the filling. The stuffed shape is then stitched to a fabric background.

The stuffing material determines the thickness of the relief pattern. For low and medium relief, use nylon stockings, cotton, wool or scraps of fabric. For high relief cotton or dacron batting, an innerlining material used in quilts works well.

The kinetic and suspended space hangings, while not new to the designer, are modified appliqué sculptures. They may move and reflect light or remain stationary.

Kinetic, or moving sculpture, dates from the ancient Greek hydro-clock and the automatic clockwork figures of the Middle Ages. Today, we see many forms of kinetic sculpture: fountains, advertising signs, mobiles and programmed constructions, etc.

Aesthetically, the same visual elements of flat appliqué (line, color, texture, shape) apply to three-dimensional sculpture. All parts, including open and closed spaces of the design, should appear necessary for the whole to exist. As with the flat wall hanging designs, three-dimensional constructions should be evaluated during creation. Look at the overall appearance, check it from different angles. Look for a relationship between the parts and the whole. Consider different surface treatments that will enhance the shape—anything from buttons, to seeds, to twigs, to cornstalks, or, even, stitchery.

Materials and Techniques

Various kinds of framework (wire, "invisible" string, dowel rods, reed, and tree branches) are carriers for the shapes. Use them as straight bars or alter the wire, dowel, reed or branch by adding pieces of like material. To create a round or angular framework, bend or shape the wire and reed. To reinforce, cover with plaster embedded gauze.

Several different materials excellent for constructing dangling forms are cloth, Pellon, starched burlaps, stitched or appliquéd forms; non-fabric materials such as wire rings, plastic or metal discs, screening, plaster embedded gauze (Pariscraft), tagboard, found objects; or any items that will dangle and float with the breeze. Find other lightweight materials known for maximum mobility.

Dangling form made of felt covered tag board accented with yarn. Student teacher, Laurel Goosman.

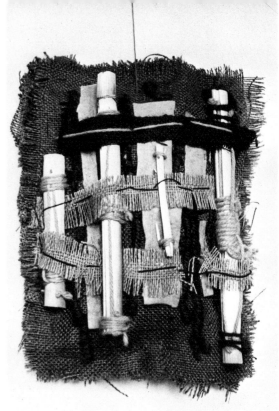

A three-dimensional construction of stuffed burlap, designed with corn stalks and accented with burlap strips and stitching. Student, Grade 4.

Burlap hanging with protruding center, accented with dangling threads. Student teacher, Laurel Goosman.

Suspended dangles inside a cut-out opening. Artist, Priscilla Sage.

Strips of fabric hang as flaps. Artist, Hans Krondahl, Sweden.

Two layers of fabric with cut-out areas in top layer exposing under layer. Artist, Jean Davies, Nova Scotia.

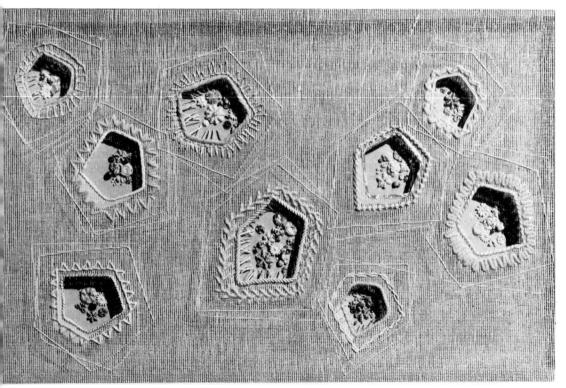

Variations

Try suspending dangles with thread or thin wire inside a cutout opening on a background fabric, or create different levels of fabric backgrounds with movable parts. Experiment with reed or wire forms, partly cloth covered, with openings that will expose dangling collections within. Let cloth hang loose or drape as part of the design. Use layers of fabric, cutting out areas of the top layer to partially show the under layer. Combine techniques (appliqué, stitchery, and weaving) letting strips of fabric, with one end stitched, hang as a flap. Use wire as a form and machine stitch over and around it to compose a lacy design. Bend the wire into a structure and suspend with string, invisible fish line, wire, or thread.

If one is intrigued with relief and three-dimensional constructions—some with transparent openings, dangles of clay, glass, or beads, and others with stuffed bumps and humps—he can discover the many different forms that will emerge when experimenting with suspended forms.

Artist, Marie Kelly.

Cloth Relief: cloth stretched over wire forms.
Student, college level. Teacher, Marilyn Pappas.
Photo, courtesy *School Arts* Magazine.

Artist, Olga Carr.

appliqué hangings   45

Abstract felt design cut into strips and overlapped to create a fringed pattern. Student, Grade 5.

Fringed pattern on a burlap background. Student, Grade 5.

Fringed appliqué hangings

Materials:
fabric
paste (Tri-Tex or glue)
scissors

Fringed appliqué, because it often protrudes from a flat background, may also have three-dimensional (low relief) qualities. It is an intriguing low relief technique to use for a hanging, especially for the enjoyment of color and the texture of a shingle-like pattern. Simple subjects, having one or two shapes, are good to try and once the process is understood, almost any subject is effective.

Procedure
The procedure for this technique is similar to other appliqué processes except for the pattern which results in a fringe design. To begin this process, plan a paper design, cutting it out to use as a guide on the fabric. For selection of fabric colors, choose one for a backing and two or more contrasting colors for the pattern. Using the paper guide, cut shapes from the fabric, edging them with glue, and paste to the background. Once the design is complete, cut it into strips of equal width and fringe along one side. Overlap the strips shingle-style, pasting along the edge opposite the fringe.

When cutting the design into strips and overlapping them, the height of the pattern will be reduced, often distorting the shape. For example, the figure of a duck, when cut and overlapped in strips, may have little or no neck. Although it is not essential to compensate for this distortion, the proportion of the original pattern can be retained by extending the figure approximately a third more in height.

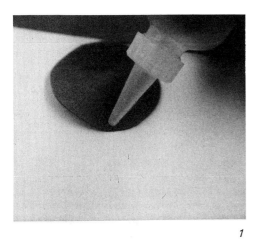

1

2

3

4

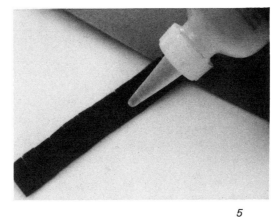

5

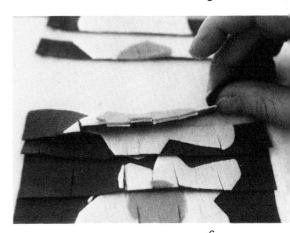

6

7

1. Cut shape and edge with glue.
2. Paste shapes to a fabric background.
3. Cut design into strips.
4. Fringe each strip by cutting along one side with scissors.
5. Squeeze glue along uncut side.
6. Overlap strips in shingle effect.
7. Completed fringed pattern.

Student, Grade 6.

Drawing with thread: design commission for child's room.

Artist, Bodil Weyde Anderson, Denmark. Lent by the Danish Society of Arts and Crafts and Industrial Design, Copenhagen, Denmark. Courtesy-Den Permanente, Denmark.

Stitchery hangings encompass a broad range of materials and techniques. This chapter provides exploration of these by discovering one's individual preference or need when creating a stitched wall hanging.

Designing backgrounds with threads and stitches

Materials:
    thread or yarn
    fabric
    scissors
    needles

In addition to appliqué, hand stitchery is an excellent way to emphasize lines, textures, and form for a wall hanging design. As a beginning, hold one end of a thread and gently let it drop onto a background fabric—a little at a time to make an interesting line. Move the thread around to make an arrangement of several lines—some moving in opposite directions, some crossing one another, and some forming outlines. Temporarily secure in place with straight pins, then a couching stitch (a back-and-forth stitch laid over each thread line) for permanent security.

stitchery hangings

Moving thread around to make a design.

Make a drawing on paper, then place a thin cotton cloth over the drawing and lightly trace the design.

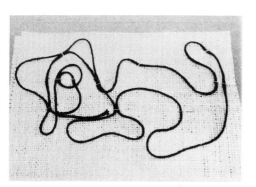

Pin thread in place then stitch in place to hold the thread secure.

Using the tracing as a guide, stitch over the lines to create a line drawing.

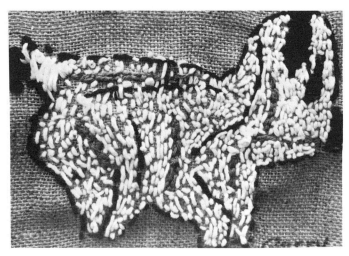

Student, Grade 3. Teacher, Betty Carstensen.

Student, Grade 3. Teacher, Betty Carstensen.

Student, Grade 4.

Experiment using thread instead of a pencil to make a line drawing. Visualize a thread composition having different lines, some interlocking at varying points and flowing in different directions. Try making a composition with a thread outline. Explore ways of making a thread pattern by running the stitches in different directions, then interweaving other stitches into them to create a surface design; later, incorporate variations of the traditional stitches.

Overlap groups of threads to mix color and create solid pattern areas, varying the direction of some threads and areas to add interest, and combining different thread weights to alter thickness. Develop mass by intertwining fibers; create tension by superimposing lines over each other; emphasize texture by building networks of lines, knots, and loops.

Variations
Be inventive with stitches. The child does this by making his own, and they can be as uninhibited as he is.

Close-up of intertwining fibers, networks of line. College Student, Betti Marchesani.

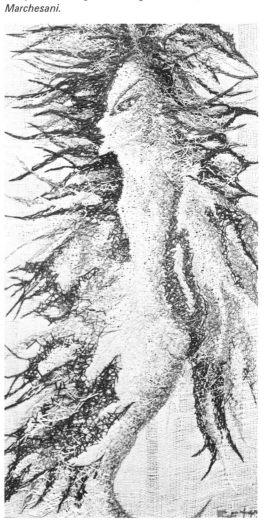

Completed design. College Student, Betti Marchesani.

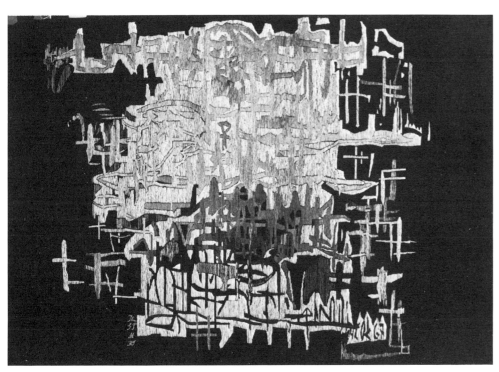

Solid linear patterns. Artist, Anna Kruse, Sweden. Photo, Courtesy Lisbeth Perrone.

Working a border design. Student, E.O. Smith Junior High School, Houston, Texas. Art Teacher, Fannie L. Holman. Courtesy *School Arts* Magazine.

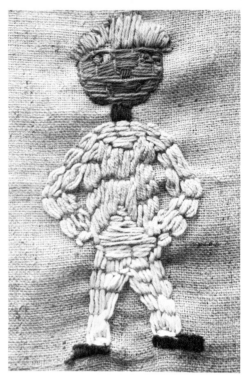

Student, Grade 6.

Student, Grade 3.

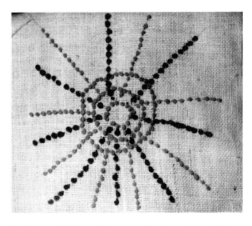

Design with French knots. Student, Grade 5.

Combine traditional with invented stitches. How many traditional stitches should one know: running, chain, buttonhole? The number is not really important. What is important are the countless variations. Improvise! One can be creative with only a few stitches—so few, in fact, that the stitch itself, its movement, and its direction suggest ideas.

One simple stitch can dominate the entire pattern. The French knot (usually a decorative additive) is interesting in its own way, having a surface texture on top of the fabric, yet making linear pattern possible with knots placed in close proximity to one another.

The ladder stitch, with its open and closed forms, creates a linear outline that can be changed in size, width, and length.

The running stitch can be a dotted line or continuous line. It can be horizontal, vertical, circular, or a combination of several directions.

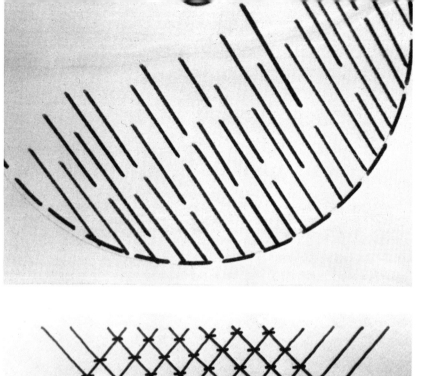

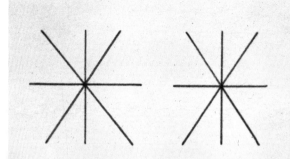

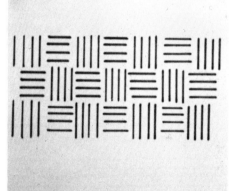

Straight line stitches made in vertical, horizontal, and crisscross patterns are simplified ways to fill or outline shapes.

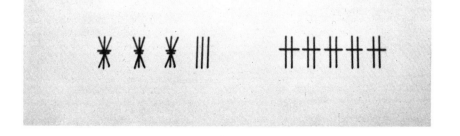

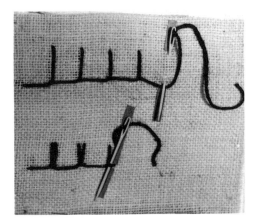

Blanket stitch.

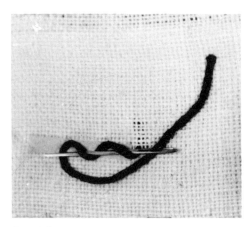

French knot.

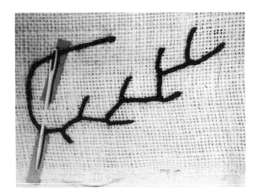

Feather stitch.

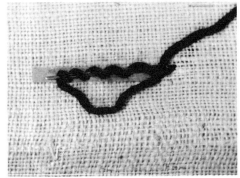

Bullion.

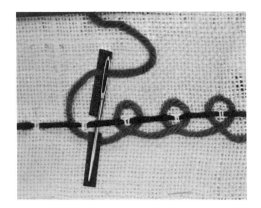

Pekinese stitch.

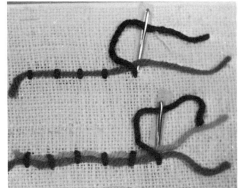

Couching stitch.

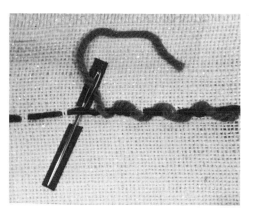

Running and laced stitches.

Satin stitch.

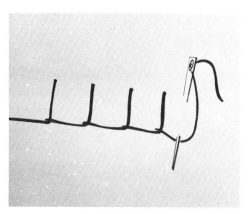

Blanket stitch.

Shading stitch.

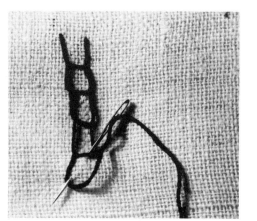

Ladder stitch.

Learning about traditional stitches

Although it is not essential to know precisely how to make the traditional stitches, some knowledge about them will help the designer when he explores and invents. An easy way to remember some of the more common stitches is to group those that are related. The blanket and feather stitch belong to the loop family; the pekinese and laced running stitch belong to the interlaced family; the French knot and bullion belong to the knotted family; and the couching and padded stitch belong to the wrapped stitch family.

These stitches form a beginning; others may be added or one can make up his own groupings. For example, one may wish to examine the interrelationships between the running stitch and the laced running stitch; the blanket stitch and the ladder stitch, etc. One might explore grouping stitches according to use. The satin stitch or French knot might be used to fill design areas; the tent, gobelin, and the running stitch for interweaving into a fabric background. The accompanying illustrations show ways stitches were used by designers to fill or outline shapes and areas of a design.

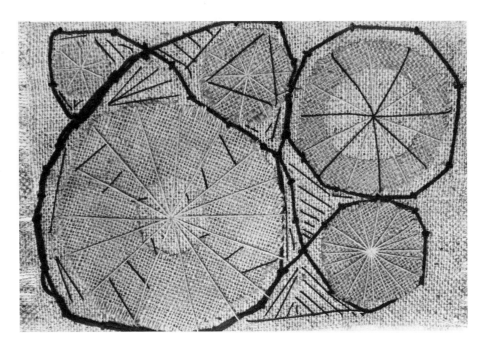

Student, Grade 3.

Student, Grade 4.

Strata: stitched lines using buttonhole, feather, and closed chain. Artist, Henry M. Stahamer AID.

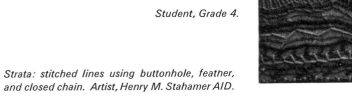

When the Shepherd comes home from the hills. Grandma Moses. Copyright, Grandma Moses Property, Inc. N.Y.

Student, Grade 3. Milwaukee, Wisconsin. Kent Anderson, Supervisor of Art.

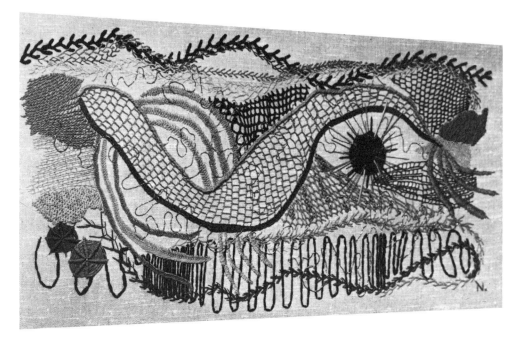

Artist, Nan Sammons.

Experiment with stitches to expand the design possibilities

- Stitches create movement

- Stitches radiate in interlocking patterns

- Stitches wander in repetitive lines

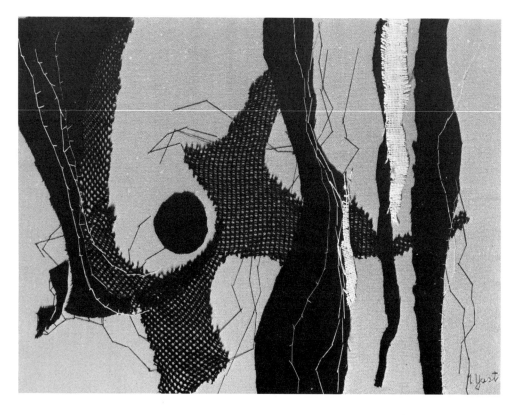

Cyclops: use of stitchery and netting. Artist, Nancy Yost.

Interlocking threads that overlap in layers, with other materials incorporated such as stones and shells. Artist, Kate Aierbach.

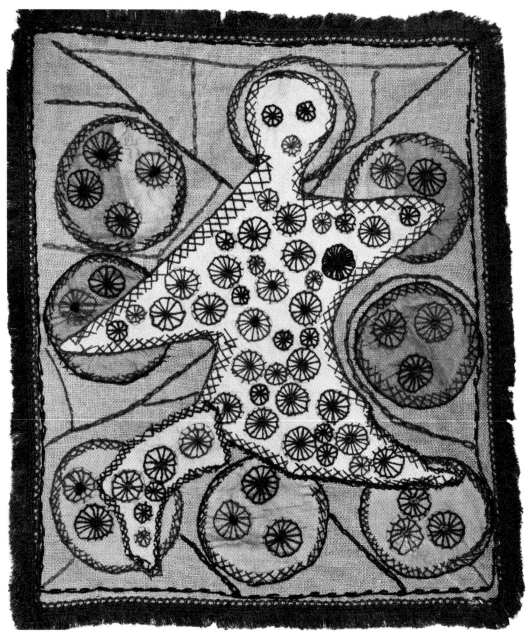

- Stitches fill areas creating textures
- Stitches outline shapes and create patterns
- Stitches create accents
- Stitches create rhythms
- Stitches distribute color
- Stitches overlap

Stitches used to fill and outline shapes. Student, E.O. Smith Junior High School, Houston, Texas. Art Teacher, Fannie L. Holman.

Artist, Birgitta Boije.

Artist, Barbro Sprinchorn, Sweden.

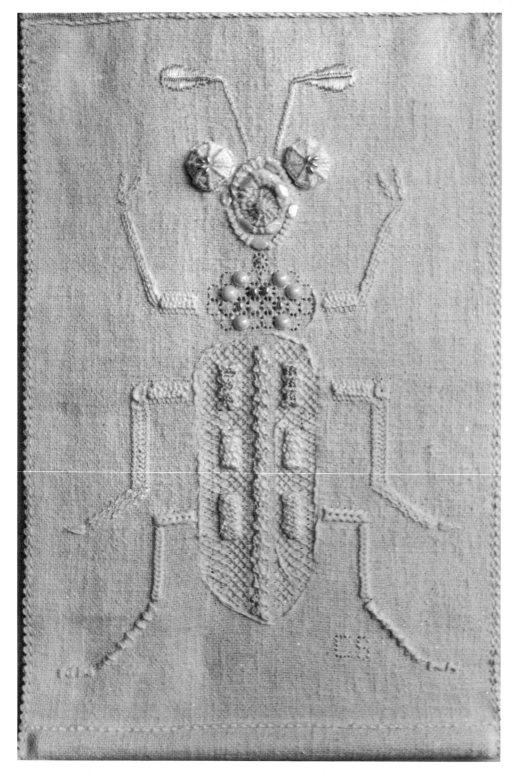

Hangings in black and white thread

Materials:
  thread
  needles
  fabric (burlap, monk's cloth)

While color is usually used in making a wall hanging, it is not essential. Modern painting has many examples of plain black and white designs (particularly in op art) where optical illusions startle the eye. In stitchery designs, one can produce dramatic effects by the stark contrast of black thread on white fabric, or white thread on black fabric, or subtle effects of white on white.

Both children and adults will find it exciting to explore pattern possibilities with strands of black or white wool on a cotton or burlap background. The simplicity of using black or white thread allows them to concentrate fully on the effectiveness of the linear pattern. The student can be introduced to the process through a variety of simple experiments:

Whitework: the use of white thread on a white background. Artist, Cynthie Sparks, England.

- Discover what kinds of lines can be made with a running stitch.

- Explore slanted, horizontal, and vertical lines, using long and short stitches.

- Create different thread patterns when filling large spaces.

- Develop different groupings of stitches.

- Create an allover pattern with thread. Make a single form and embellish it with thread.

- Repeat lines, emphasizing and varying the length of stitch.

- Prepare thumbnail sketches of imaginary scenes: city streets, boats, mountains, groupings of animals, insects, people, illustrations for stories or songs. Then, transfer into a black or white thread design.

Black and white thread patterns can resemble a form of embroidery popular during the 16th century. Although different from a drawing, the technique was known as blackwork, or Spanish work, and was prevalent in many European countries. We have few actual examples remaining today, but portrait paintings of the period often show elaborate blackwork designs adorning costumes of men and women, especially the collars, cuffs, and ruffled shirts.

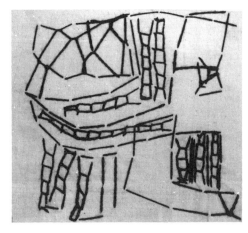
Contrast of black thread on white fabric.

City scene. Student, Grade 7. Baltimore, Maryland. George F. Horn, Supervisor of Art. Richard Micherdzinski, Director of Art.

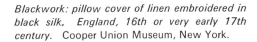
Blackwork: pillow cover of linen embroidered in black silk. England, 16th or very early 17th century. Cooper Union Museum, New York.

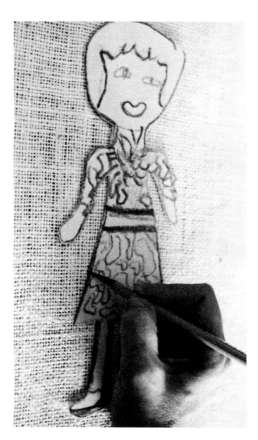

Transferring the design to fabric. Student, Grade 5.

Rows of straight lines in the top of dress identifies the body and arms. Tone is changed by the use of straight line stitches in contrast to inverted "V" shaped stitches.

Emphasis on tone, showing contrast between closely and widely spaced lines. Student, Grade 6.

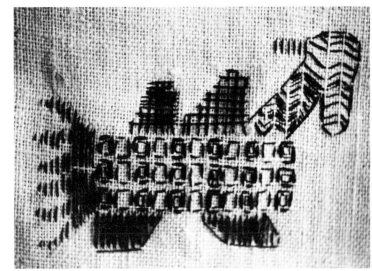

Counted thread pattern.   Student, Grade 5.

Procedure

It is evident when looking at some blackwork that the evenness of background threads determines the clarity of the design. When selecting fabrics such as linen, monk's cloth, or burlap, make sure you check the evenness of weave before purchasing. Burlap, especially, must be checked, because it comes in both semi-even and uneven weaves. Regardless of the woven state, burlap is an inexpensive background for children. It is easiest for them to count the threads when it is stapled or tacked to a frame. An alternate method is to pull every so many threads (every fourth thread) both vertically and horizontally to make the thread pattern clearer to see. Still another background possibility is plastic screening, a non-cloth material.

Although counted thread stitching may be done spontaneously, a preplanned shape will help guide the beginner when working out his idea. Once the design is drawn on paper and cut out, he can draw around it with pencil, then experiment with different counted thread stitches, selecting those best to fit the design. Repeating rows of the same stitch will help the design take shape.

Blackwork thrives on simplicity—simplicity of stitch, design, and tone. The repetitive design resulting from the counted thread pattern should appear distinctly to the eye. One using the blackwork technique should emphasize tone—values of light and dark grays. Stitches spaced close to one another appear darker than those spaced farther apart.

But one can change the tone of the design in other ways. Different weight threads will change the tone, and the shape of the stitches themselves (V-shaped, curved, slanted) will create other tones. Repeating a single stitch in one section of a design creates still another tone.

Variations

Experiment by making stitched patterns with threads that vary in gradations of value. Try using contrasts—of black and white; try adding threads of middle value; or experiment with several gradations between black and white.

Blackwork stitches are good for filling large background areas. Try some of the following:

• Make a pattern of squares. Link these together with vertical and horizontal lines. Fit these squares in the open space.

• Create a pattern of lines crossed in different directions. Link them together with long slanted lines.

• Prepare a group of cross-stitches.

• Make several rows of running stitches, altering the placement of each row.

Be inventive; discover different design possibilities by stitching over varying numbers of background threads.

Experiment with contrasts of the same color thread and fabric—chartreuse thread on a dark green fabric; light blue thread on a dark blue background. Combine the techniques of drawing with thread and counted thread stitching.

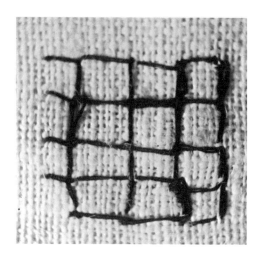

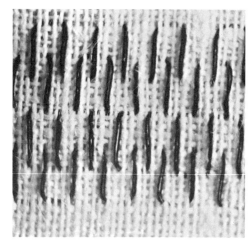

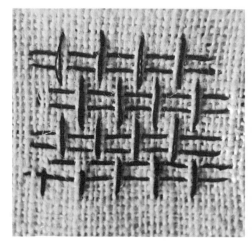

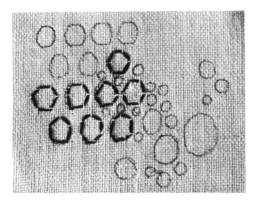

Using counted thread as a drawing technique. This design was first drawn with a felt marker as a guide.

Blossom: a free counted thread design spacing the thread to make different gradations of black tones.

Detail of Blossom.

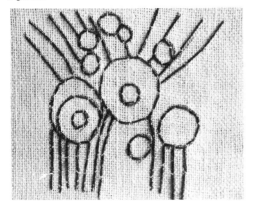

Counted thread drawing.

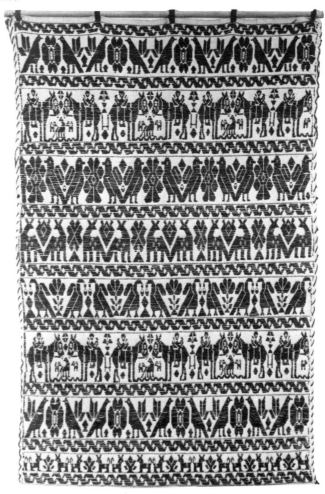

Counted thread: Mexican. Collection of the Author.

Hangings in crewel wool

Materials:
  crewel wool (a substitute is wool yarn
  that can be separated into thinner strands)
  needle
  scissors
  fabric

Crewel stitchery offers innumerable
possibilities for those who like to use
different color shadings in their wall
hanging designs. The word crewel means
a thin, two-stranded worsted wool.
Crewel, sometimes called ''Jacobean embroidery,'' was especially popular during
the 17th and 18th centuries for exhibiting
pictures on walls or easels and for embellishing chairs, bed coverings, pillows, and
clothing. Many of the designs were floral
and fruit accented with birds or animals,
and surrounded by flowing line patterns.
In the 17th century the few wool dyes
available were made from weeds, leaves,
roots, and bark.

Today, crewel stitchery is used for a
different purpose. The time and expense
of embroidering bedspreads, curtains, and
clothing make these activities impractical,
so the designer often turns to wall hangings that are purely aesthetic. Patterns for
these hangings can vary from simple
forms to complex groups of forms.
There is no limit to the subject matter
which may include motifs of animals,
insects, birds, flowers, leaves, landscapes,
plus abstract designs. The pattern may
take up part of the background fabric and
expose other parts or cover the background completely.

Winter Birds. Artist, Mrs. Huge M. Parrish.
Photo, University of New Hampshire Photo
Service.

Crewel, worked over a background surface. Kashmir, India. Collection of the Author.

18th Century (English). Piece: crewel embroidery, flowers in rose with some yellow, leaves and stems soft blue, worked chiefly in chain stitch, on cream twill ground. Wool on cotton. The Metropolitan Museum of Art, Anonymous Gift, 1949.

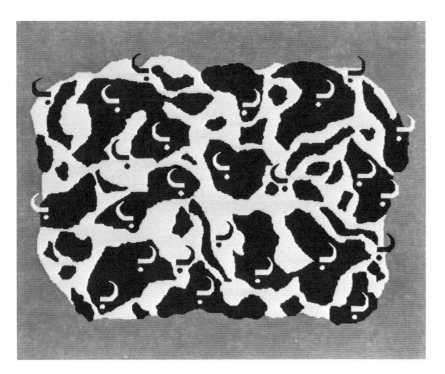

The Herd: straight gobelin stitch worked in horizontal rows on coarse linen. Artist, Alberta Small Strauss.

Crewel worked over entire background. Artist, Alberta Small Strauss.

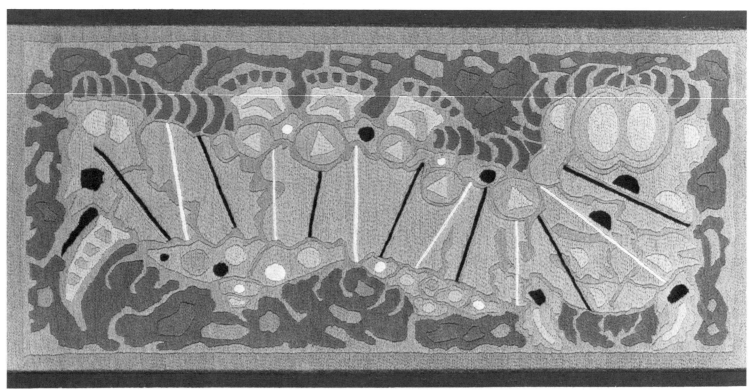

One can now buy crewel yarn in many colors and shades to create forms with subtle gradation, or of one color in varying tones and used singly or in combination with a related color. One can also vary the weight of the yarn: by using different thicknesses, separating strands, adding strands, or combining wool strands with other threads such as silk. If crewel wool is not available, a simulated crewel design can be made by substituting regular yarn and separating its strands. This is a desirable method if cost is a factor when making crewel designs in the school program.

Whether child or adult, one should be willing to experiment with color, thickness of wool, and technique, and be ready to make unexpected discoveries in the course of his work. He also should take time to investigate and evaluate his discoveries, thereby measuring the range of aesthetic effects in his hanging.

Procedure

The designer might think of himself as a painter: the background is the canvas, the yarns, splashes of color. The advanced designer (child or adult) may wish to plan the pattern on paper before stitching it to the background. After he is satisfied with the pattern, he may draw it onto the background fabric using one of the following methods: draw the plan on paper with a transfer pencil, then place the design face down, ironing it from the paper to the background; trace around a cutout pattern, or use carbon paper.

Many different stitches may be used for crewel embroidery. Two useful stitches illustrated here are chain and blanket. Others are illustrated in the section, Designing Wall Hanging Backgrounds with Threads and Stitches.

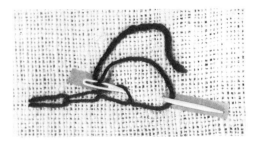

Chain stitch

Blanket Stitch

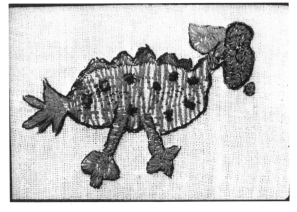

Student, Grade 6.

Forest Games: crewel worked over part of background. Artist, Wilanna Bristow.

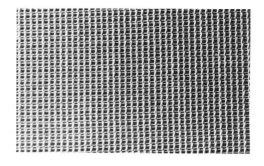
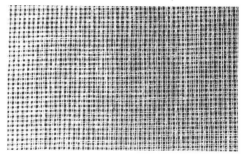
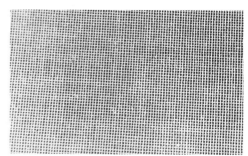
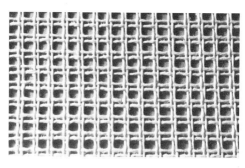

Canvas stitched hangings

Materials:
  needle (selected to fit a mesh back-
    ground with an eye opening larger
    than a strand of wool)
  thread (silk, for fine meshes only)
  canvas (select the size of mesh de-
    sired)
  scissors
  thimble (optional)
  frame (optional)

Children and adults find canvas hangings easy and enjoyable to design with
yarn. The backing, usually called cross-
stitch canvas or rug backing, is an open
mesh material similar in texture to wire
screening. It, along with other kinds of
canvas, is available in a selection of
mesh sizes, 5–40 threads to the inch.
The stiff, yet flexible canvas has a starched-
like quality giving it body and making it
usable without a frame. Stitching into a
canvas background strengthens and
decorates the canvas. The stitches are
worked over and around the mesh
threads to produce the design.

*Exposed background is part of design. Student,
Grade 8. Niagara Falls, New York, Art Teacher,
Larry Bell.*

Student, Grade 6.

Student, Grade 6.

Garden Plot: raffia, knitting wool, covered button molds; experimental canvas work. Artist, Patricia Langford, Australia.

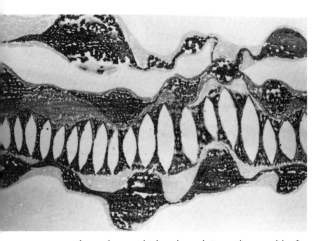

A predrawn design in paint used as guide for example below.

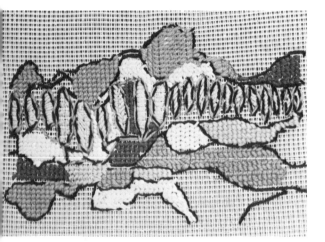

Above design interpreted in canvas embroidery. The exposed mesh may be left as is or covered with stitches.

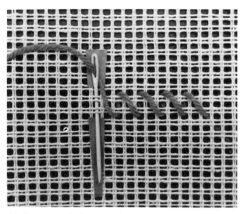

Half cross-stitch.

Tent stitch.

Gobelin stitch.

Needlepoint

Dating back to the 16th century, needlepoint or English embroidery is a sophisticated canvas embroidery. It has all the color qualities of an exotic wool embroidery, yet looks like a woven tapestry. Commonly used on chair seats, cabinets, valances, clothing and purses, and in pictures, an example is an elaborate scene on linen, embroidered in wool tent stitch and silk needlepoint.

Needlepoint, as a decorative element, found its way to America during colonial times. Today, it is one of the many needle techniques employed by the contemporary craftsman.

Specifically, needlepoint embroidery means covering a mesh canvas with thread or wool. The size of mesh, the number of threads per inch, whether single or double thread, determines the name of the embroidery: petit point, needlepoint, gros point, or bold point.

Linen embroidered in wool tent stitch (some areas in silk needlepoint). England, late 16th-early 17th century. The Cooper Union Museum, New York.

To make a petit point, choose a mesh of 20 threads to the inch or smaller; for needlepoint, choose a mesh of 14–18 threads to the inch; and for gros point, choose a mesh of 8–12 threads to the inch; for bold stitches, choose a mesh of 5–7 threads to the inch.

Design drawn on canvas with a felt-tip marker: motif of turtle made with vertical stitch. Student, Grade 6.

Procedure

The start for general canvas stitchery and needlepoint is similar. Experiment with different stitches and matching weights of wool on small pieces of canvas. Notice how the stitches and canvas respond to one another.

How many different stitches should one use? Although there are many, three common ones are the half-cross, tent, and gobelin. Explore these and other stitches to find one that is just right for the design. Use it, even if it's the only stitch in the whole design, or make the design in one stitch and the background in another.

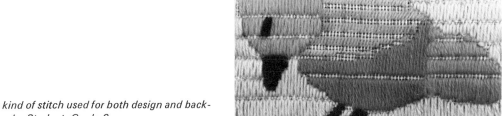

One kind of stitch used for both design and background. Student, Grade 6.

Artist, Vivian Steinberg.

After deciding on the stitches and the color of yarn, work out a motif, or let the motif suggest the stitch. There are several approaches to try when making the design. Before stitching, draw a design on the canvas with a felt tip marker; lay the canvas over a predrawn design and trace it with a marker; or randomly group various patterns of stitches. One might translate a painting or a section of a painting on canvas.

When the needlepoint is complete, straighten the canvas by blocking. See section on blocking for procedure.

Painting. Artist, Miriam Shorr.

Needlepoint design interpreted from painting. Artist, Miriam Shorr.

Variations

Try different fabric backgrounds for a wall hanging in place of mesh. Use coarsely woven fabrics. Superimpose nets and transparent fabrics over the canvas. Combine needlepoint stitches and inventive embroidery. Combine different weight yarns. Experiment with different ways to accent a design:

• Add stitches on top of previously made stitches such as chain, French knot, couching, ladder.

• Vary the pattern of the hanging; use raised stitches for parts of the design and flat stitches for other parts and the background.

• Combine dull and bright colored strands within the same pattern (metal, wool, silk, raffia).

Appliqué shapes to the canvas; fill in open areas with needlepoint.

Consider some of the following questions when making a hanging: Should all the canvas be covered with stitches or partially exposed? Can other materials—fabrics, leathers, and buttons be added to canvas embroidery? What advantage does stitching on canvas have over stitching into a tightly woven cloth? Can machine stitching be part of the design? How will one stitch look when repeated several times?

Different stitch patterns made with raised and flat stitches. Artist, Miriam Shorr.

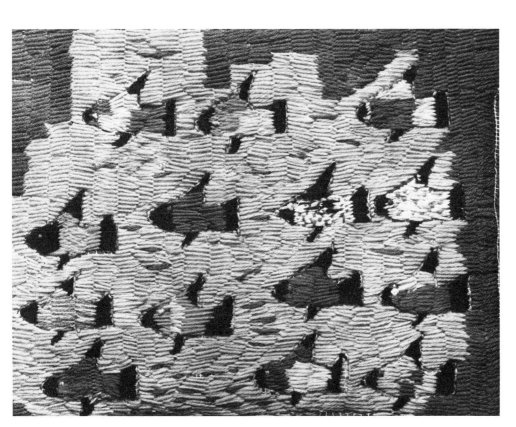

Mesh background completely covered with stitches. Student, Grade 8. Niagara Falls, New York, Art Teacher, Larry Bell.

Green Onions. Artist, Elizabeth O'Leary.

Hangings with machine stitched threads

Materials:
  sewing machine
  thread
  fabric
  scissors

In the past, the designer of wall hangings did most of his stitchery by hand. Today, he uses both hand and machine. Like hand stitchery, machine stitchery is another way to draw with thread. A design may appear as a freely sketched drawing (with linear patterns that flow in different directions) or a massive textural shape. Using the machine requires an imaginative individual, willing to experiment while he masters the tool and makes it work for him.

There is no need to learn all the mechanical details of the machine. However, a general knowledge of tension control will add to the effectiveness of the stitching. With this understanding about thread tension and a desire to try different methods of machine stitchery, little or no technical information is necessary for the beginner to become adept.

Selecting a Machine
One doesn't need the latest model sewing machine to do effective machine embroidered hangings. Any straight needle machine, although limited in number of stitches, is a beginning tool for a stitchery adventure. In fact, the straight needle model will encourage students to use stitches of different lengths imaginatively for creativeness. Attachments will produce a great variety of stitches.

Student, Grade 5.

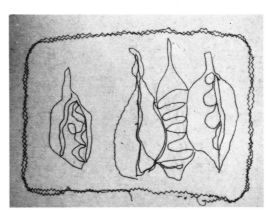

Student, Grade 5.

Student, Grade 6.

Experiments with stitches. Artist, Dolores Negele.

Photo courtesy Helen Rose, Supervisor of Art, Richmond, Va.

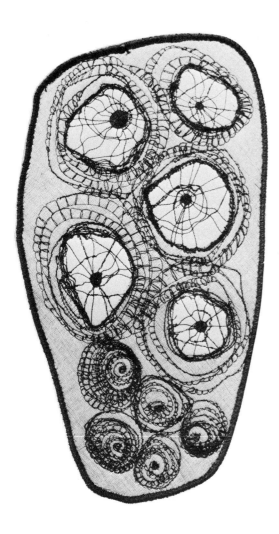

Machine stitchery and cut-work. To make outer edge of the shape, zigzag a stitch over a wire to hold it in position. Any fabric extending beyond the wire form is cut away. Artist, Jean Davies, Nova Scotia.

The tension adjustment

- Make a linear pattern with the tension set for regular sewing.

- Add tension on bobbin thread to distinctly space the stitches.

- Add more tension to top thread for solid line patterns.

Try other design variations

- Stitch lines close together but vary the space between them.

- Use several threads in the same needle.

- Stitch one color of thread over another.

- Use contrasting threads in needle and bobbin.

- Stitch back and forth across cutout openings (for lacy effects).

However, when students use a swing needle and multi-stitch machine, they are able to work with more stitches—the number depending on the model of the machine.

Procedure

Regardless of which machine is used (the straight needle or the multi-stitch), experiment with:

- Try the quilter guide to make rows of stitches the desired distance apart.

- Use the stitch adjustment lever to create variations in length of stitch.

- Explore possibilities of the cloth guide.

- Remove the presser foot to make circular, vertical, and horizontal movements. (When foot is removed, bottom stitches are loose and top stitches are tight.)

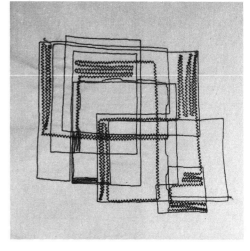

Simple forms made with few stitches.

Using an embroidery hoop, the designer may make a linear pattern, repeating different decorative stitches to develop the design. When one area of the design is completed, the hoop is moved to another part of the cloth.

Notice that the stitching is done without the presser foot. To keep the cloth from crumpling when the presser foot is removed, depress the drop feed or insert a protective plate over it, using an embroidery hoop to hold the fabric taut.

The designer may stitch on a felt background. By holding the felt taut, stitching will be easier and smoother.

Machine stitchery and cutwork may be combined. For this kind of work, use tight tension for the upper thread, a loose tension for the lower thread.

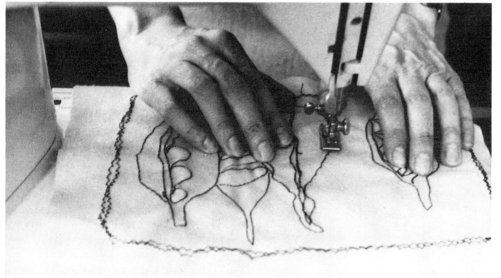

Stitching on felt.

In the following illustrations, fabric shapes were machine stitched to a cloth background. For detail, the artist stitched lines moving in different directions over the design.

Try other machine variations:

• Try stitching on a lace background.

• Stitch with a heavy thread; add cut-work for accent.

• Stretch different size mesh or net (hair-fish net) over a wool or cotton background, then machine stitch over a design.

• Stitch a scene.

• Machine stitch a design and accent with yarn.

• Make a machine-stitched fabric collage.

Pattern made with machine stitchery and yarn.

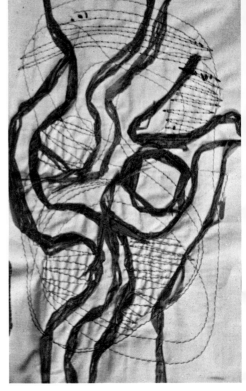

Machine stitchery over lines of raffia.

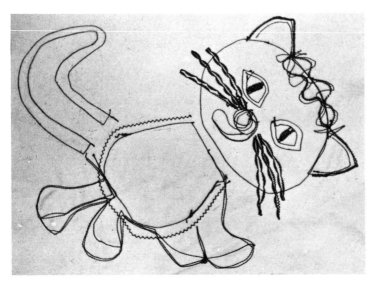

Stitched thread drawing showing the back side of Cat, Cat.

Cat, Cat: a machine stitched appliqué accented with stitching.

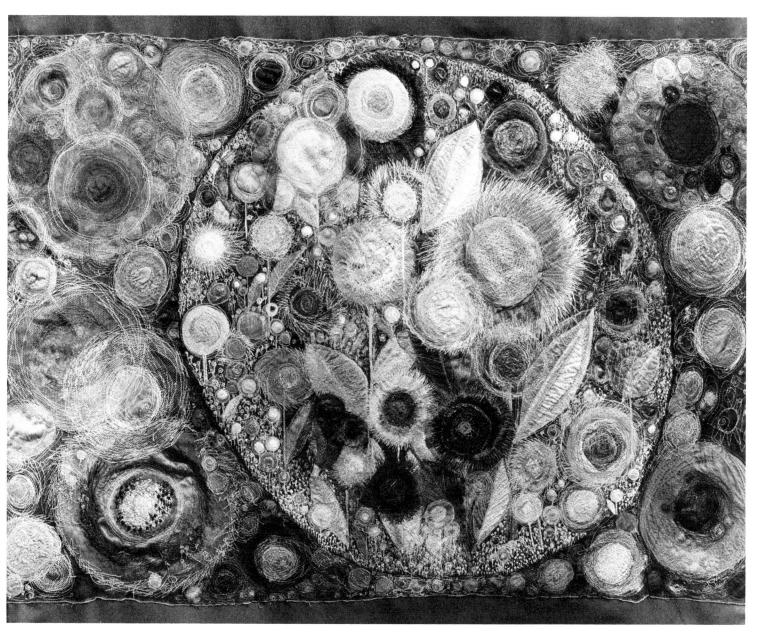

The Moon.   Artist, Ruth Salinger, Holland.

Laurel Leaves. Shelburne Museum Inc., Shelburne, Vermont.

Quilted hangings

Materials:
  fabric of cotton or silk
  filling of cotton, dacron, flannel
  thread (#50–60 or, for fine work, #80)
  scissors
  needle
  thimble (optional)

If one likes to experiment with old techniques, quilting is an interesting way to make or accent a hanging.

Quilting was brought to America by the English and Dutch in the 1700s and quickly became one of America's most popular folk arts. Many examples of early American quilting still exist—mostly in folk art museums. Designs on many of these quilts were often influenced by the country of origin of the designer; for example, Pennsylvania Dutch (Design Medley) and French (Laurel Leaves). Personal preferences of early quilt makers were demonstrated in the motifs: birds, animals, family, flowers, words, and Civil War themes.

It took many hours to make a bed size quilt, so the quilt maker often invited neighbors to contribute designs and to help stitch the quilt. These neighborly gatherings, called "quilting bees," were also a popular way to socialize.

Design Medley. Shelburne Museum Inc., Shelburne, Vermont.

Civil War Counterpane. Shelburne Museum Inc., Shelburne, Vermont.

Crazy Quilt. Shelburne Museum Inc., Shelburne, Vermont.

Many early quilts suggest subject matter that would interest the school-age student and inspire him to create quilt hangings emphasizing personalized motifs. The subject matter of these quilts emphasizes that ideas are limitless. In fact, the quilt itself can symbolize one or several themes simultaneously.

For teaching, organize groups of students to design a quilt for a wall hanging; or use the technique of quilting for parts of a wall hanging pattern. A quilted wall hanging can be large or mini-size. Or, quilt small pieces and stitch them together into a large panel, or attach quilted pieces to another design for decorative accent.

Quilting is the technique of using three layers of material together—top, interlining, and bottom. The top and bottom may be composed of the same or different fabric, while cotton batting, dacron polyester fiber fill, or flannel are ideal for the in-between layer. Stitching through these layers with tiny running stitches (either by hand or machine) holds the layers together, and at the same time, allows the unstitched parts to puff up. Quilting creates high and low surfaces that make sculptural-relief patterns. As an art form, quilting differs from other kinds of embroidery by depending on surface embellishments with thread. Different kinds of interlinings alter the thickness of the quilt and change its sculptural appearance.

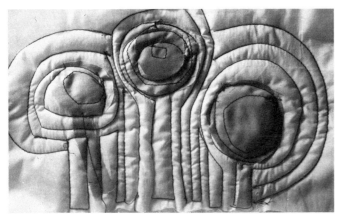

Appliquéd pieces of fabric and quilting.

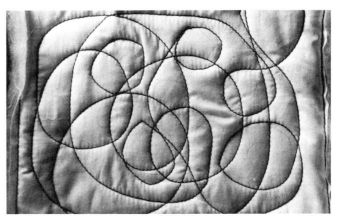

Stitches made with dark thread.

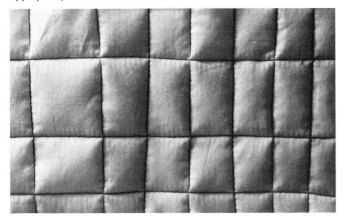

Dacron polyester lining creates high surfaces.

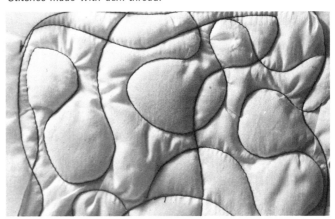

Larger areas give "puffy" effect.

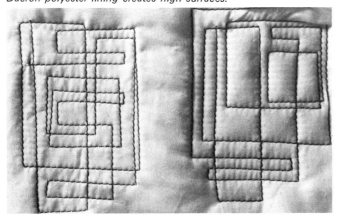

Experiments with stitchery on two types of inter-lining. Acrylon interlining used for design on right; cotton batting used for design on left. Acrylon lining creates puffy effect.

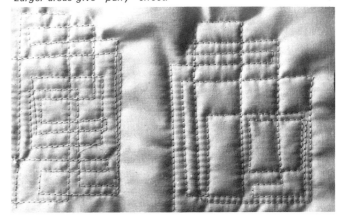

Stitches made with white thread on a white fabric, and a cotton (left) and acrylon (right) interlining.

A design is planned on paper.

Planning the design

To make the coverlet or top layer of the quilt, simply appliqué, piece fabrics together (patchwork), block print, or crayon a design.

Think about the ways to use quilting before beginning a design. Will it be an appliqué pattern on a quilted background or small pieces to accent another appliqué and stitchery hanging?

Plan the size of the hanging in advance. The quilt may be any size depending on the desired result. As a beginning, try quilting material for a background. Cut small pieces of fabric to appliqué on top of the quilting. Use simple easy-to-cut outlines and allow extra material along the edges for hemming. When cutting multiple shapes of the same design, sandpaper or cardboard makes an effective pattern guide. Vary the design by quilting the background after the design is applied or quilt both the design and background.

The design is cut out and used as a pattern when cutting the fabric.

Procedure for quilting

Cut two pieces of fabric the same size to make a top and bottom for the quilt hanging. Arrange a cutout design on the top layer of fabric and baste it in place. Hem edges of the design, stitching through all layers with a tiny quilting stitch (a running stitch that penetrates the top, inner, and bottom layers). Develop the relief pattern of high and low surfaces by quilting the design and background. To make large shapes lie flat, stitch outwardly from the center.

The design is appliquéd to a quilted background.

Variations

Some variations to quilting are similar to the padding effects in the basic quilting technique. Trapunto, a stuffed rather than a quilted design, gives a higher relief. For this technique, use the same materials as in quilting but only two layers of fabric. Place the two layers on one another, then, sewing through both layers of fabric, outline with stitches shapes that will be filled.

Another stuffed variation having a decorative potential is cord quilting. Using fabric top and bottom, stitch two parallel lines to form a channel (the width between the parallel lines depends on the thickness of the cord). With a large eye needle, bobby pin, paper clip, or wire, pull the cord through the channel. For channels that curve and wander in different directions, a needle works best. Where necessary, insert this needle through the fabric, snaking the cord around the curves inside the channel.

Piece: quilted in type called trapunto work. XIX Century American 1812. The Metropolitan Museum of Art, Gift of Mrs. John G. Pennypacker, 1957.

Cord work.

Still another variation is a quilt top composed of silhouette shapes similar to snowflake designs. This type of quilt pattern is known as Hawaiian quilting with interesting potential for both children and adults. By folding paper in different ways and cutting out areas, a fascinating design will emerge. If, when the paper is unfolded, more cut work is necessary, re-fold some parts and add more cut work. Tissue paper works best for a paper pattern; it easily folds for cutting. For a guide, use the paper when cutting fabric. Place the design on a thin cloth, possibly batiste, follow the creases in the paper and refold the paper with the cloth. Once the design is cut, pin the cloth to a fabric background. When all pieces are pinned in place, secure with stitches.

Other variations are possible by embellishing the quilt design: embroider the unquilted appliqué shapes of a quilt, embroider parts of a quilted hanging, combine quilting, trapunto and cord quilting.

Hawaiian quilted banners.

Artist, Helen Bitar.

The Urge To Grow: queen size quilt. Designed by Artists, Charles and Rubynelle Counts; executed by Rising Fawn, Georgia Craftsmen. Photo, Edward Du Puy.

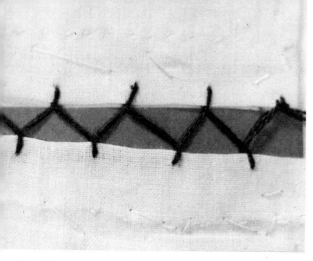

Fagoting.

Decorative treatments add interesting detail to the wall hangings we have been discussing. Try these:

Fagoting is a technique that laces two pieces of fabric together, thereby combining decorative accent with practicality.

Smocking is a pattern produced by different arrangements of "gathers" (pulled fabric along a stitched line to create puckers) in the fabric. Voile, batiste, lawn, or silk are excellent soft-textured fabrics for smocking. Scraps of these fabrics may be used for creating small patterns.

The solid line stitch may appear contemporary, but its origin is traced to Egypt. This stitch is worked in one direction then back again in the opposite direction—to fill between stitches.

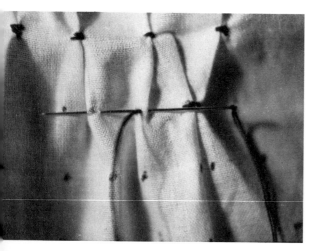

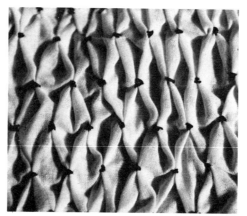

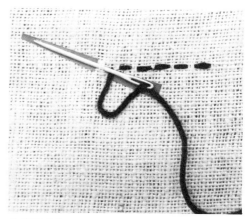

A dotted line.

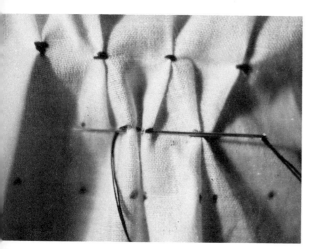

Smocking.

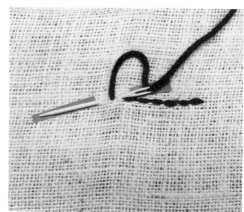

A solid line.

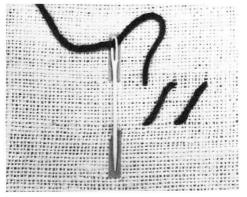

The cross-stitch, traced to the Coptic period of ancient Egypt, is a popular stitch for filling large areas. Make a slant stitch in one direction, then make a second slant stitch to cross in the opposite direction and over the first one.

Teneriffe describes a stitch practiced on the island of Teneriffe (the largest of the Canary Islands). For this stitch, think of a spider web. Make long stitches that radiate from a center point. Weave a thread under and around the long stitches to give an over-and-under spider web appearance.

decorative treatments

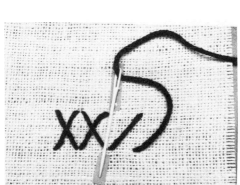

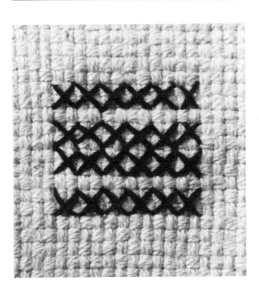

A variation of the Assisi technique: different colors of yarn used to make cross stitches on a pulled thread burlap. Student, Grade 7.

Assisi embroidery, an embroidery still practiced in Italy, is a specific kind of pattern made as follows: the shape is outlined in very dark thread; the background surrounding the design (filled with a lighter shade of thread) is cross-stitched to silhouette the shape; it is varied by reversing the cross-stitching, filling the pattern with cross-stitches instead of the background.

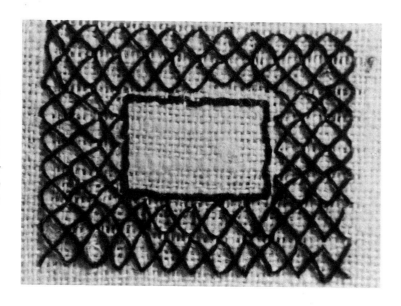

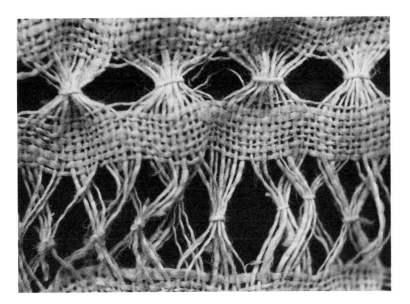

Drawn stitchery is a method of withdrawing threads from a background fabric (either the horizontal threads or vertical threads) and weaving over and under a contrasting color or weight of thread. The pattern is altered by tying or stitching groups of vertical threads together in different positions.

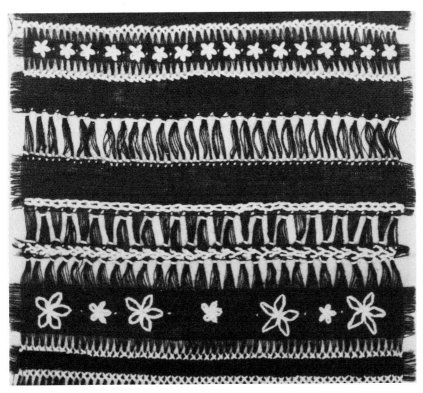

Weaving into fabric works well with coarse, loosely woven fabrics. Huck, burlap, and monk's cloth are ideal, but other material such as onion and potato bags are workable too. The pattern is made by weaving over one thread and under two; weaving under two threads and over three; or weaving over and under any number combinations of threads.

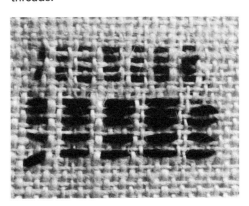

Pulled thread and stitchery.   Student, Grade 7.

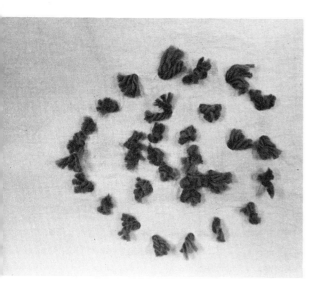

Candlewicking, an American folk art and, generally known today as chenille work, is less than 200 years old. During colonial times the candlewicking process was a common way to decorate bed coverings, curtains, pillows, and robes. Today it is one of the many ways to beautify and accent a wall hanging by blending a technique of the past with that of the present.

Originally, candlewicking was done with a thread called candlewick cotton—a thick, multi-ply thread, but today this thread is seldom available. Substitutes are four-, six-, and eight-ply threads. Such threads as Lily four-strand filler, and others of varying plies, can be added to or taken apart to make a thread of any desired thickness.

Large eye needles are necessary to carry the several thread strands; needles made especially for candlewicking have wide shafts and double eyes (one beneath the other) to carry multi-ply threads.

For this technique, choose a washable, shrinkable fabric to tighten and hold the stitches securely in place. When candlewicking a total hanging, materials should retain their color and body during the washing process. When candlewicking small sections of a design, candlewick separate pieces of cloth and add these to a background that does not need washing.

A suggested method for stitching is as follows: Outline the design with loose, but evenly spaced running stitches. With scissors, cut the threads of each stitch at its center. Soak the completed design in warm soapy water, then rinse well and shake but do not wring out. Let dry but do not iron. The cut threads should fluff into tufts.

Accents, the details that make the design striking must be sensitively used to enhance the total pattern. Accents should provide emphasis and contrasts to the general pattern, or even clarify a design. Many different kinds of material may serve as accents.

Beads.

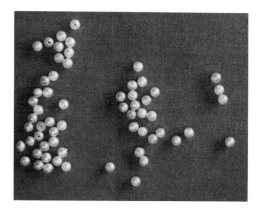

Beads.

Glass beads.

Metallic shapes.

Clay shapes with stitchery.

Metallic shapes.

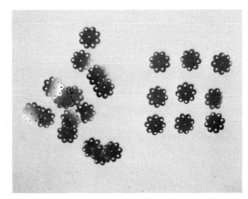

Metallic shapes.

Bone suspended on thread.

Metallic shapes.

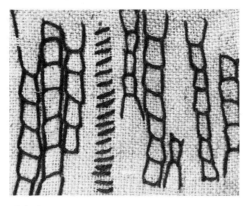

Stitches.

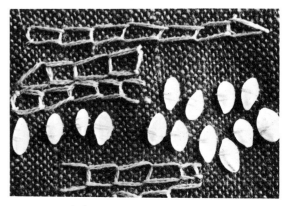

Seeds and stitchery.

Bells, copper foil, wool, and felt. Artist, Patricia Malarcher.

Beading. The Cooper Union Museum, New York.

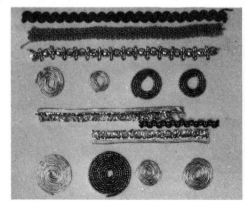

Edgings, metallic and beaded cords.

There are a great many approaches to designing a hanging. Inspiration may come from many sources. One designer may emphasize material, another stitches. Still others will concentrate on subject matter or invent new ways to portray an idea. Each person must find his own approach. This section illustrates a few approaches and encourages the reader to search and discover his individual way of working.

varieties of approaches

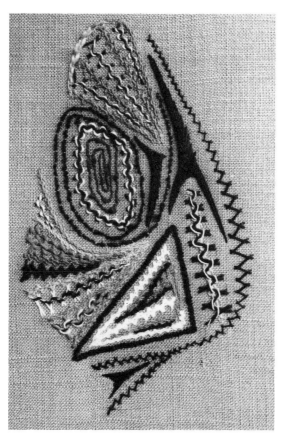

A single pattern approached in different ways: a stitched design. Artist, Cynthie Sparks, London, England.

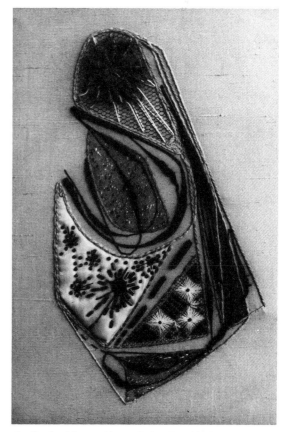

Appliqué with couching. Artist, Cynthie Sparks, London, England.

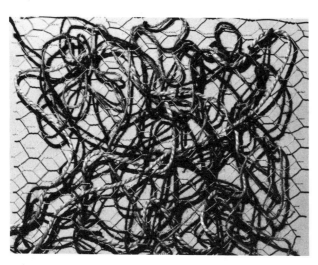

Jute and chicken wire.

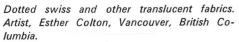

Dotted swiss and other translucent fabrics. Artist, Esther Colton, Vancouver, British Columbia.

Daisy: raffia combined with net, wool, and thread. Artist, Nadine Turner, Australia.

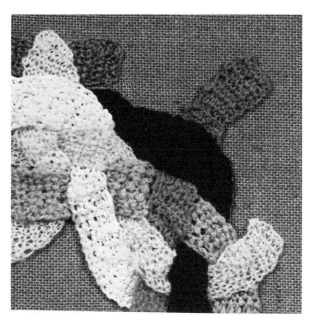

The inner workings of a Gordian knot: detached buttonhole stitch. Artist, Jill C. Jackson.

Stitches:

Line designs using straight, stem, coral knot, and crested chain stitches. Textures with detached buttonhole stitches.

Different size feather and chain stitches.

Chain and crested chain stitches combined.

Contours made with thread.

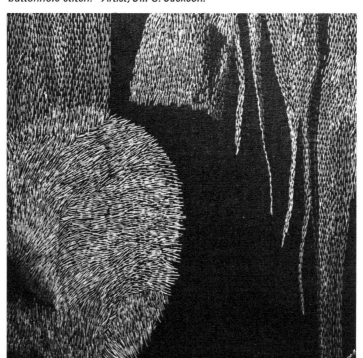

Patterns in thread. Artist, Grete Schioler.

Tree of Life: silhouette pattern. Artist, Marie Hauge, Norway.

• Pattern with thread and fabric

• Silhouette

• Different backgrounds

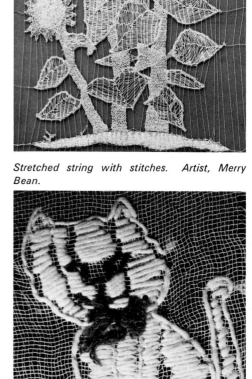

Stretched string with stitches. Artist, Merry Bean.

Stitchery on cheesecloth. Student, Grade 7. Birmingham, Alabama. Art Teacher, Mabel Thompson, Supervisor of Art, Lila Wells.

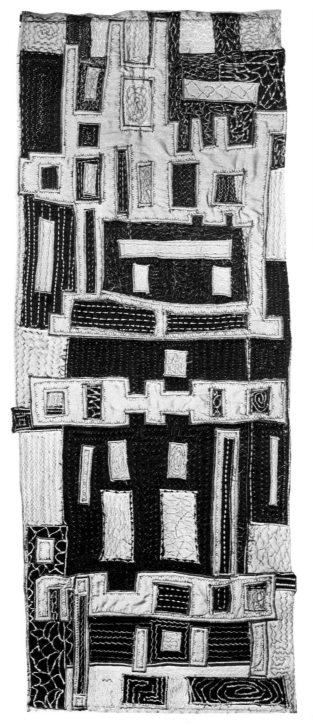

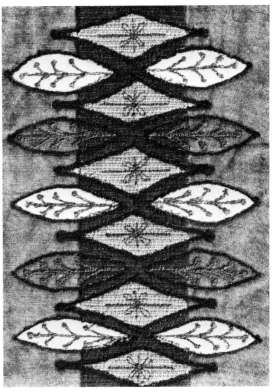

Appliquéd stripe overlaid with black organdie. Some areas cut out to reveal the underlying color. Artist, Jean Davies, Nova Scotia.

Machine stitchery as accent. Artist, Dolores Negele.

Pieced background of different fabrics using open and closed areas. Artist, Birgitta Boije.

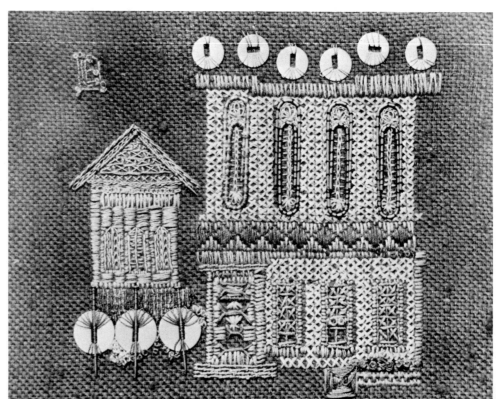

Stitchery accented with metal washers and paper clips. Artist, Elizabeth M. O'Leary.

104

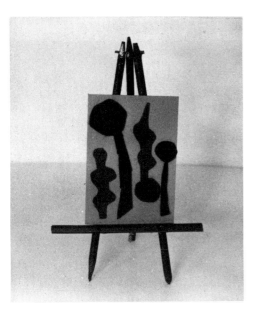

Reversible hanging that dangles from a string: cardboard sandwiched between layers of felt. Student, Grade 6.

Hanging displayed on easel. (Photo far left) Student, Grade 6.

Mini-hangings

Not all hangings need be large. Some people like to design small hangings— even hangings of mini-size—but large enough to portray an idea. For example, try a tiny 2″ x 3″ design and mount it on a mini, 5″ high easel; or make several small hangings and place them, as a series, on the wall.

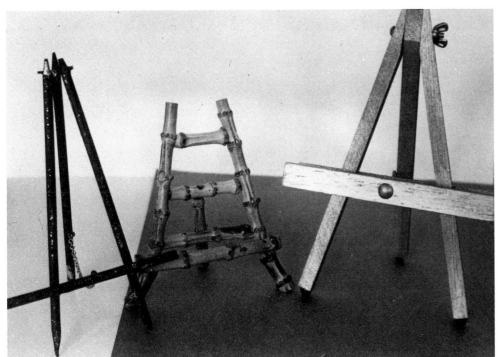

Different kinds of easels, 3 to 6 inches high.

Materials for mini-hangings can be carried in pocket or purse, making it convenient to work on the hanging at any time. Miniature hangings are handy for the traveler who is short on space and time.

Student, Grade 5.

Student, Grade 4.

Student, Grade 7.

Student, Grade 7.

Yarn painting, "Tabla", is the Mexican art of pressing strands of yarn into a beeswax coated background. Two effective substitutes for beeswax are white glue diluted with water or polyvinyl acetate adhesive. These, when brushed evenly over small areas on a cardboard or cloth background, dry clear leaving no stain on the yarn design.

Yet another substitute for beeswax is contact paper. Because this paper is sticky on both sides, one side can be adhered to fabric, heavy cardboard, or fabric covered cardboard; a drawing made for a guide on the exposed side; and the yarn pressed into place.

Still a further method of making a yarn painting is to trail the glue into desired areas before pressing the yarn.

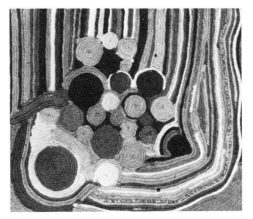

Student, Grade 7.   Bloomfield, New Jersey.
Art Teacher, Dolores Negele.

yarn painting

Student, Grade 7.

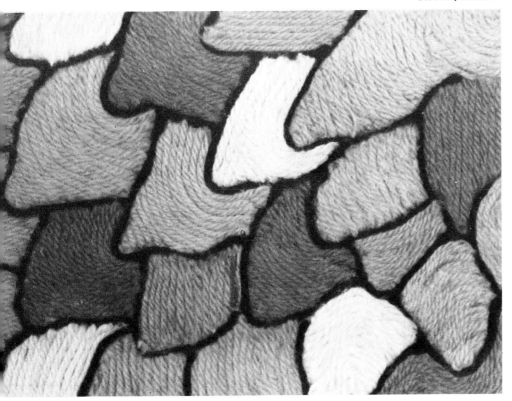

Student, Grade 3.

Felts, burlap, and printed cotton stitched to a
burlap background. Student, Grade 4.

Cut fabric shapes being pasted to a fabric background. Faith Girdler, Grade 2, Old Greenwich
Conn.

Left—
*Pasted fabric accented with lace on burlap back-
ground. Student, Grade 3.*

Right—
*Felt pasted to fabric background: yarn made into
puff balls makes the eyes and nose. Student,
Grade 2.*

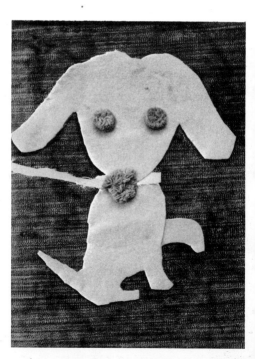

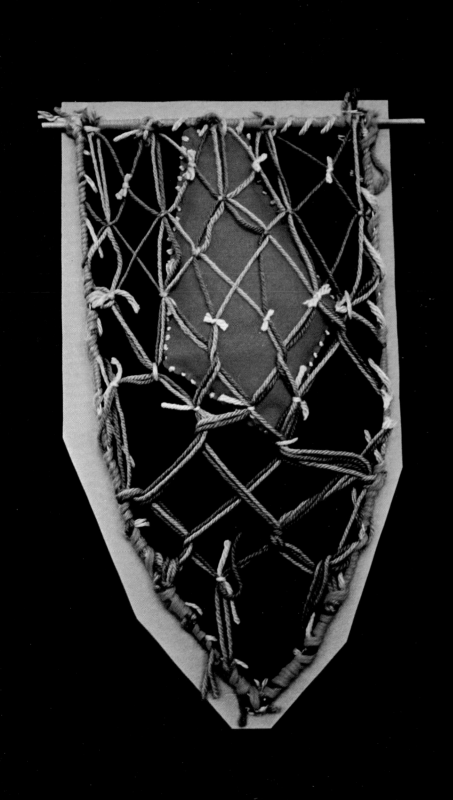

colorful
hangings
by students

Knotted yarn worked over top of stuffed appliqué.
Student, Grade 7.

Scraps of fabric overlapped and accented with stitchery. Student, Grade 4.

Felt appliqué illustrating a child's imaginary idea of a house. Student, Grade 3.

Appliqué and stitched pattern, using felt and printed organdy. Inspired by the inside of an apple. Student, Grade 4.

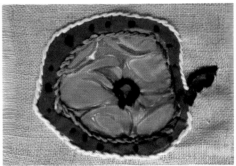

Appliqué and stitched pattern. Inspired by the inside of a watermelon. Student, Grade 4.

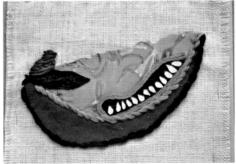

Stitchery on burlap. Student, Grade 4.

Roving glued to a burlap background using the mono-rub technique. Student, Grade 1.

Cord glued onto a background of newspaper and burlap using the mono-rub technique. Student, Grade 7.

Jute glued to burlap using the mono-rub technique. Student, Grade 5.

Stuffed appliqué shapes mounted on dowel rods that are inserted into a branch. Student, Grade 7.

Pasted appliqué. Student, Grade 7.

Stitched animal. Student, Grade 3.

Fringed appliqué. The Three Pigs. Student, Grade 3.

Pasted appliqué. Inspired by the opera of Hansel and Gretel. Student, Grade 4.

Stitched scene. Student, Grade 5.

Stitchery by Peruvian child. Collection of Joyce and Ted Lynch.

Many of the techniques and materials previously discussed may be combined to make collages, assemblages, banners, or simplified moiré patterns. On the following pages these hangings are discussed and illustrations provided to inspire further exploration into the world of wall hangings.

Collage hangings

Materials:
  fabric
  found materials (paper, variations of
    cloth, cardboard)
  glue
  scissors
  needles
  yarn or thread

Collage, from the French word *coller,* means to stick or paste. When thinking of a collage hanging, immediately envision a number of different materials (paper, cardboard, and cloth) cut and pasted to a background.

Such hangings will delight children, for they love to cut and paste. They quickly put their ideas into tangible design, using braids, ribbons, fabrics, rug yarn, and puffs of cotton. This process encourages children to explore textures and materials through their senses of sight and feel. In fact, collage is often the avenue to new awareness of one's surroundings, new insights to design arrangements, and new sources of self-confidence.

Notice how adept the child is with collage materials. He combines magazine pictures with felt and cotton to organize patterns of color and texture; he incorporates various kinds of cloth (corduroy, cotton, felt, burlap, lace) to make simple patterns and shapes.

innovative combina-tions

Magazine pictures and felt. Student, Grade 2.

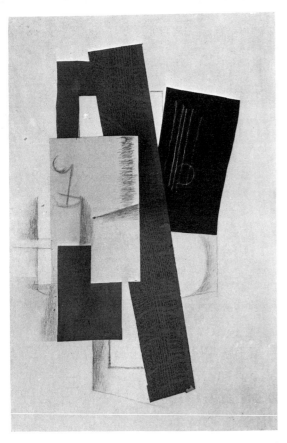

Guitar (1913-14): oil on canvas, with pasted paper, pencil, chalk, 39¼ x 25-5/8". Collection The Museum of Modern Art, New York. Acquired through the Lillie P. Bliss Bequest.

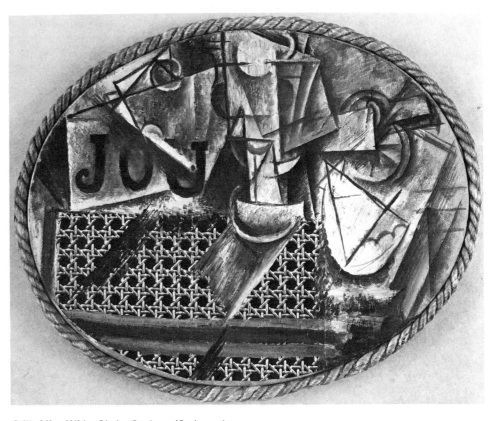

Still Life With Chair Caning (Paris, winter 1911,12): oil, pasted oilcloth simulating chair canning on canvas, 10-5/8 x 13¾" oval. Permission S.P.A.D.E.M. 1970 by French Reproduction Rights Inc. and The Museum of Modern Art, New York.

But the practice of cutting and pasting materials is not limited to children. In fact, it is practiced by students at all levels as well as professional artists. One of the most significant collage works of the late 19th and early 20th centuries was the cutout valentine.

Two artists who influenced contemporary collage are Braque and Picasso. In one of Braque's most notable examples, ''Compotier'' or ''Fruit Bowl,'' he pasted decorative wallpapers (simulated wood grain) to a sheet of paper, sketched over it with charcoal, later adding more wallpaper. In his example, ''Guitar,'' he combined papier collé (pasted paper), pencil and chalk with oil on canvas.

Unlike Braque, who worked mostly with plain and corrugated papers, Picasso

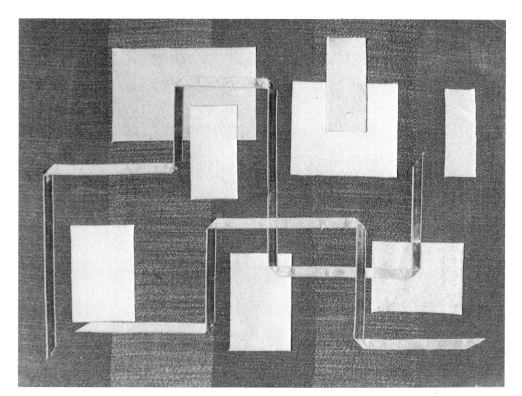

Post cards cut into different sizes, covered with silk fabric and pasted to a cloth background. Artist, Mary Pilcher, England.

with an innovative spirit employed many different materials, including wood, tin, sand, and fabrics. In his painting "Still Life with Chair Caning," he painted alphabetical characters, used oilcloth to represent the caning, and rope to frame the design. Yet, in his later examples, he simulated the rope by painting its likeness.

Influenced by Braque and Picasso, many artists have used the collage techniques in their work. But they expanded the materials to include laces, ribbon, braids, bottle labels, postcards, toothpicks, sawdust, and cutout advertisements, to name only a few. Students should study these and other collage works to determine which material will best portray their ideas and feelings.

Paper advertisement torn into strips then applied to linen fabric and combined with a buttonhole, closed chain, and free stitching. Artist, Henry M. Stahmer, A.I.D.

Procedure: look for materials

Knowing there are thousands of items at our fingertips, we should try to "see" as opposed to "looking,"—to analyze, discriminate, and select as we choose colors, textures, threads, and non-fabric items to make effective designs.

The use of collage materials ranges from single bits of fabric to combinations with non-cloth materials. Some specific collage combinations are:

• gauze combined with string and newspaper

• woven textures with patterned fabrics

• batiked cloth with coarsely woven cloth

• cheese meshes with cotton prints

• solid canvas with mesh canvases

• plastic and cloth tapes with cloth covered forms made of wires and cardboard

• fabric covered cardboard

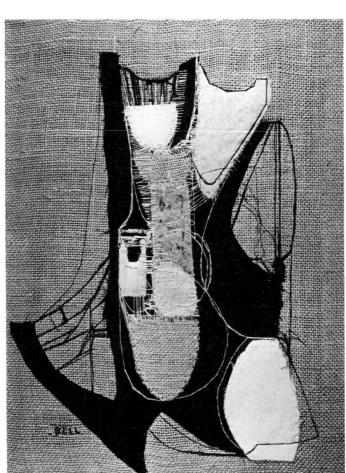

Woven textures with cotton fabric and stitchery. Artist, Larry J. Bell.

The Bee and the Garden: collage of feathers, felt, sequins, fringe on background of velvet. Student, Amy Girdler, Grade 3, Old Greenwich, Conn.

Choose a technique

Some basic collage techniques are cutting, pasting, tearing, and smoking. The hanging itself may be made with any one or a combination of these techniques.

Cutting is a common technique and the most prevalent way to make a collage hanging. Tearing, as a technique, makes an interesting frayed thread texture. Some fabrics respond more readily to tearing than others. Smoking parts of fabric alters its appearance; burning and scorching are other ways to add variety. Other useful techniques are rubbings (by transferring a relief pattern) and montages (compositions made of pictorial fabrics). If we wish to make a collage hanging, incorporating several collage techniques, we may partially paste the materials in place and later secure them with stitching.

Students will soon find their own methods and develop personal styles by experimenting with different materials and adhesives. But one approach that is simple and direct is the block-in method: Cut pieces of fabric and arrange them into a silhouette kind of design. Overlap and repeat color, pattern, and texture to unify the composition. Define some of the shapes by outlining edges and filling shapes. For further detail, add bits and pieces of contrasting fabric and non-cloth materials.

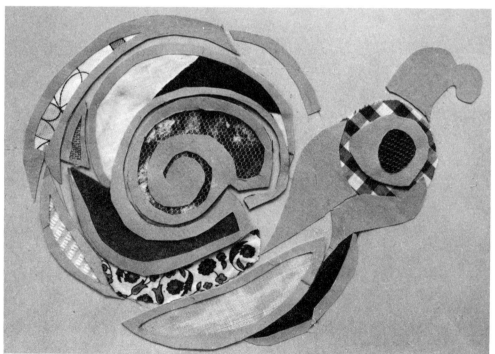

Cut felt with net and printed cotton inserts. Student, Grade 7.

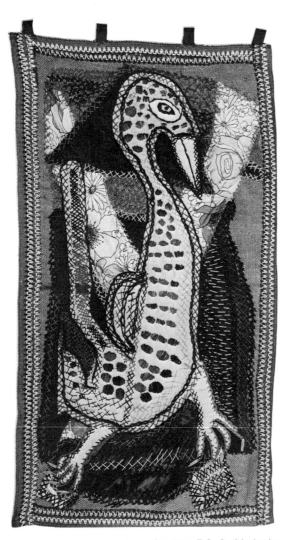

Burlap and ravelings. Student, Grade 7.

Invitation to Spring. Student, E.O. Smith Junior High School, Houston, Texas. Art Teacher, Fannie Holman. Photo courtesy School Arts Magazine.

Aesthetic aspects of collage

Despite previous experience in other media, the pattern possibilities inherent in collage must be kept in mind if the novice is to have a rich experience in this medium. Problems presented for the first time to the beginner should familiarize him with space relationships, tactile experiences, and pattern organization. Some of these problems should encourage him to notice what happens when placing fabrics over one another, between one another, and juxtaposed to one another; to feel and touch surfaces; and to experiment with wrapping and crumpling of fabrics. When collage is approached as a problem-solving design experience, the often hodgepodge conglomeration of materials becomes an organized pattern.

To further experience some problem-solving experiments, try the following:

• Make textural compositions. Strive for variety in texture, fabric, and color; accent with machine and hand stitching.

• Develop a design of open and closed shapes with superimposed gauze stretched across the background of appliqué forms.

• Make a series of designs showing variations of contrasts and comparisons:
1. strips of different fabrics in overlapping patterns
2. strips of different colors in overlapping patterns
3. strips of fabric elevated at different levels

• Explore varying relationships—a pattern of different colored cottons or decorative cotton prints combined with batik, tie-dye, or stitchery.

• Create designs that show contrast between texture, color, and pattern; positioning of fabrics on different plane levels; and simulated textures of living things (fish scales, bird feathers, shells of turtles). Accent with decorative sequins, leather, and straw.

Burlap and ravelings.   Student, Grade 7.

Student, Grade 1.

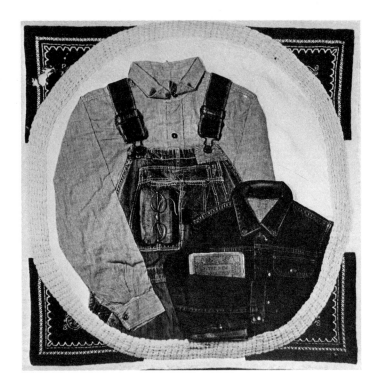

Bullitt County, a fabric portrait: everyday articles of overalls and jacket, a shirt, bandana handkerchief, eye glasses and case and a third grade McGuffey's Reader stitched to a heavy cotton background. Artist, Alma Lesch.

Assemblage hangings

Materials:
   found items (cloth, jewelry, wood)
   scissors
   glues
   fabric

Assemblage is an extension of collage, which along with paper, cardboard and cloth, includes bark, buttons, and wood. These constructions might incorporate any of the design elements of shape, space, and rhythm. They are either two- or three-dimensional, often emerging as relief or free-standing sculptures that reach out to the viewer to attract his attention. The focus in assemblage is upon the common elements normally unnoticed in life: socks, vests, gloves, jewelry, metal, stones and other kinds of found materials. With little change, except for a fold, drape, or a crumple, these familiar items are useful to the creator for making unusual and appealing design statements.

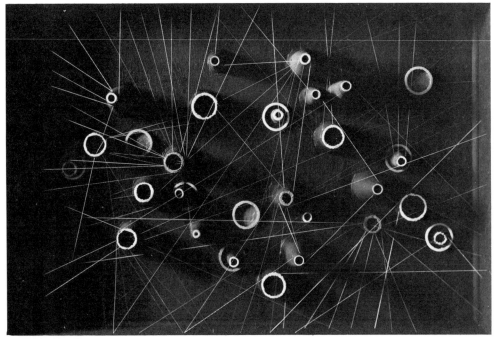

Twenty First Century: a thread sculpture of threads stretched from cardboard cones. Artist, Nancy Yost.

Who would expect an assemblage hanging to be made with an old shirt, a McGuffey reader, eyeglasses, or a collection of buttons? Such assemblages stretch the imagination—challenge the designer of any age to collect, experiment, and react to his materials.

Sturdy burlaps, monk's cloth, and the like make suitable backgrounds for an assembled design. Strong bonding adhesives such as ply-a-bond, iron glue, and acrylic mediums also are necessary.

The procedure for making or constructing an assemblage is not difficult. One approach is to assemble items and arrange them to make a pattern. To vary, introduce collage materials. No special techniques are necessary but some of the wall hanging techniques previously discussed will prove useful when attaching pieces and parts of things in your assemblage design.

Since assemblage is an extension of collage, many of the aesthetic aspects of an assembled design are similar to those of collage construction. Try some of the experiments suggested for collage hangings, and other items for the flat, two-dimensional materials. For example, a jacket with folded sleeves and turned up collar, substituted for a piece of fabric; different size circles and cones substituted for different strips of fabric; painted cardboard on different planes combined with fabric and Styrofoam.

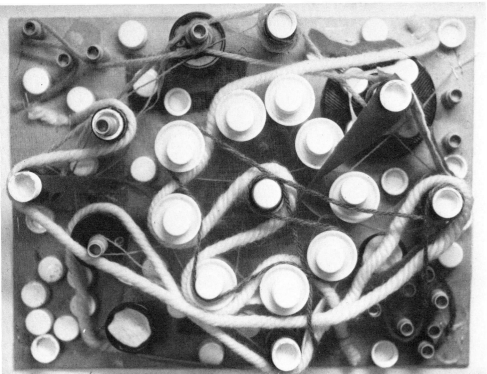

College student, Ruth Donakowski.

At work making banners, Niskayuna Public Schools, Schenectady, New York. Art teacher, Virginia W. Mills.

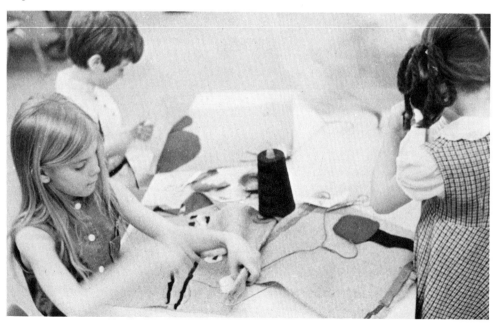

Banners

Materials:
  fabric (felt, burlap, Indian head)
  scissors
  glues
  thread and yarn
  needles
  sewing machine (optional)

Although simple wood standards of various kinds resembling signs were first used in Egypt, the word banner reflects back to the cross-bearing flags of the Crusades and the knights of the Middle Ages. Flags, streamers, and pennants were often used to identify guilds, nations, noblemen, celebrations, and religious and political organizations. Today, banners in the form of flags identify states, nations, localities, organizations, bands, athletic teams, etc. But, interestingly enough, the banner has other roles in pop art, advertising, gallery announcements, new motion pictures, plays, and similar events.

The banner is really a poster made of fabric, basically presenting one idea. The image is simple, and bold, crystallizing the artist's idea in a short, concise visual statement.

Flag in green and tan. Dutch XVII Century (1652). The Metropolitan Museum of Art, Rogers Fund, 1912.

In addition to the numerous ideas suggested for previous appliqué and stitchery hangings, banners may:

• pictorially symbolize portraits of people, animals and clowns

• fictitious ideas (talking animals, fairy tales)

• myths and legends

• everyday objects (books, toys)

• nature (trees, leaves, acorns, flower blossoms, weeds, grass)

• insects (butterflies, caterpillars)

• musical instruments

• transportation (trains, airplanes, automobiles)

• religious themes

Student, Paterson State College, Wayne, New Jersey. Courtesy, Dr. Joyce Lynch, Professor of Art.

innovative combinations   119

Banner designs may be abstract or representative in subject matter. The theme should attract the viewer's attention by emphasizing the image in various ways:

- make the image large or bold

- repeat it in size and color

- combine different fabric materials

- use bold outlines to emphasize certain sections

- experiment with dramatic color contrasts and subtleties

- interject words, letters, or numbers

Procession: felt collage. Artist, Rozsika B. Blackstone.

Birdland U.S.A.: birds and houses repeated in different sizes, shapes, and colors. Artists, Joyce and Ted Lynch.

To make a banner, choose a technique in any of the previous chapters. Refer to the suggested materials or experiment with new supplies.

A banner design may be approached in different ways. Here are ways to get started:

• Try using simple road sign symbols on a contrasting background.

• Cut simple bird or animal shapes and overlay with long strands of thread or yarn.

• Draw a large insect, tree, or house form; outline and fill with one stitch such as the ladder stitch. Appliqué fabric shapes on background surrounding the stitched shape.

Student, Paterson State College, Wayne, New Jersey. Courtesy, Joyce Lynch, Professor of Art.

Headboard banner. Artist, Dolores Negele.

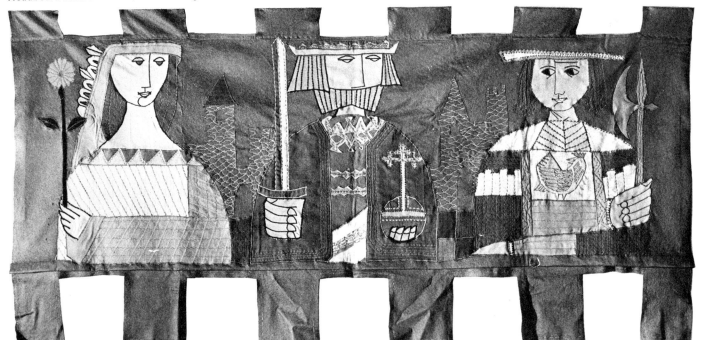

A linear design made as a preliminary sketch for a thread pattern.

Optical hangings

Materials:
 fabric
 thread
 scissors

In the drama of man and his environment, the artist of today explores many avenues to make life meaningful. One such avenue is optical art—a tantalizing play on the eye with color, line and shape. These moiré effects (irregular, wavy or ripple patterns) or optical illusions, keep the eye busy jumping from color to color or line to line, often emerging as distorted images.

Riley, Bridget. Current. 1964. Synthetic polymer paint, on composition board, 58⅜ x 58⅞". Collection The Museum of Modern Art, New York. Philip C. Johnson Fund.

OP III: wool on canvas. Artist, Polly Goodman.

Appliqué pattern of felt triangles on fabric of mixed fibers. 16½" x 26". Artist, Patricia Malarcher.

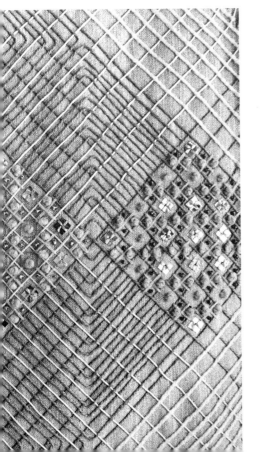

Detail: wool, jute, linen and synthetic threads with pieces of mylar on Belgian linen. 70" x 55". Artist, Patricia Malarcher.

innovative combinations   123

Students can make simplified moiré patterns by experimenting with imaginative checkerboard shapes, fine patterns that interrupt, converge, and intercept one another, and color arrangements. Many of the appliqué or stitchery techniques are applicable as long as the design becomes an optical pattern.

Student, Grade 5.

Imaginative checkerboard pattern made with crayon as a study for optical design. Student, Grade 5.

Burlap ravelings and cotton print. Student, Grade 8.

Sunburst: wool yarn worked on cotton in optical pattern.

A preliminary sketch in crayon.

Other combinations

There are many and varied combinations one might use to make a hanging. Combinations of different kinds can challenge the imaginative mind to search, explore, and experiment. The following examples illustrate a few of many possibilities among the vast array of materials and techniques used by designers.

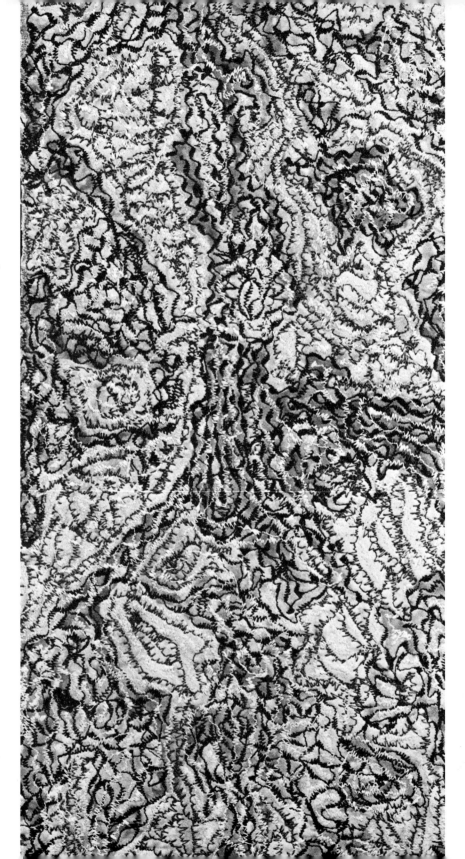

Batik and machine stitchery. Artist, Dolores Negele.

126

Tin can lids and stitchery. Student, Grade 5.
Art Teacher, May Kedney, Oneonta, New York.

Printed fabric and crayon. Student, Wayne
Miller, Grade 2, Columbus, Ohio.

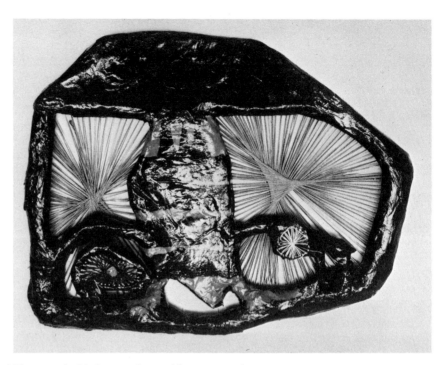

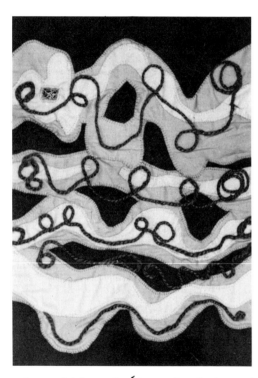

Plaster embedded gauze form with woven and
stretched threads. Student, Grade 8.

Stitchery on tie-dye. Student, Paterson State
College, Wayne, New Jersey. Dr. Robert Cooke,
Professor of Art.

Cotton fabric appliquéd to velvet background
and accented with jute. Preplanned in a cray-pas
design. Student, Grade 6.

Stitchery over silk-screen print. Artist, Patrick Dearborn.

Woven and knotted threads

Fibers and threads are often woven or knotted to make a hanging. Processes for weaving and knotting are available in a number of reference books, some of which are listed in the bibliography. The examples shown here should stimulate one to further explore this area of expression.

Student, Grade 5.

Student, Grade 7.

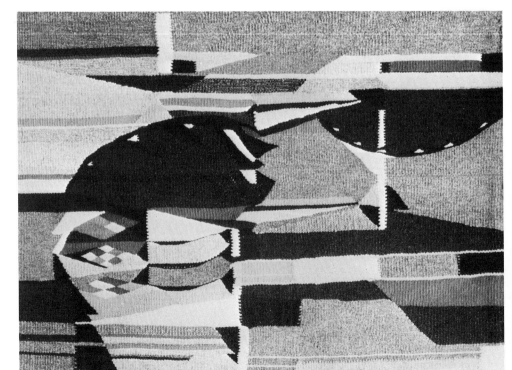

Grey Light: Artist, Randi Hoaas, Norway.

130

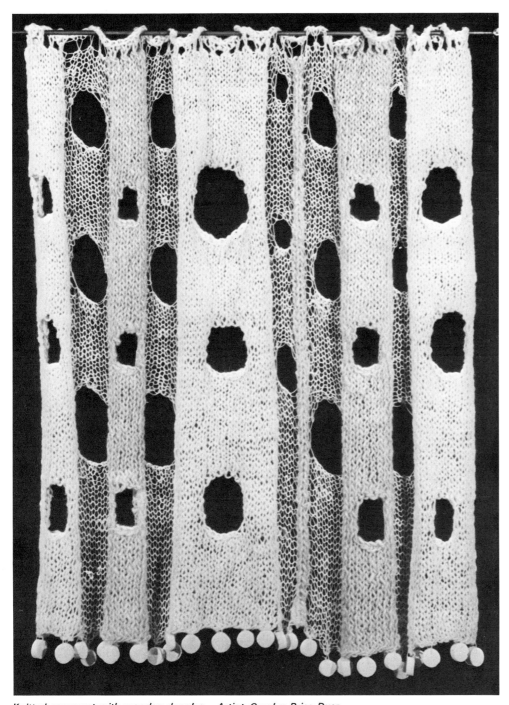

Artist, Grete Schioler.

Knitted casement with wooden dangles. Artist Carolyn Price Dyer.

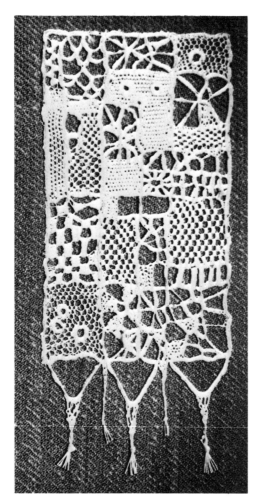

Crochet. Artist, Bucky King.

Hooking, knotting, stitchery and window shade pulls with drawn threads at top. The Nature of Materials. Artist, Alma Lesch.

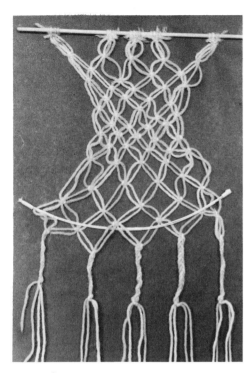

Macramé. Student, Grade 7.

Thread networks and knotting suspended in frame. Artist, Lucia Suffel.

Artist, Sally Adams.

Artist, Martha Miller.

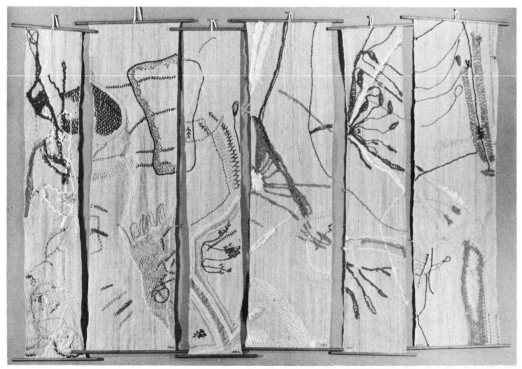

There are several ways to avoid wrinkles, bumps, and warping of fabric—changes in the appearance of the design which often make the hanging look out of shape. Two effective ways to compensate for these conditions are to steam iron the hanging, or block it as follows:

• Place the completed design back side up on a wood or wallboard surface and dampen it with a wet sponge.

• Stretch the fabric until it appears taut, holding it in place with rustproof tacks. (Allow to dry before removing tacks.)

• Lay a damp towel over the back of the hanging and press it with a hot iron. The hanging is now ready for mounting.

Mounting

Mounting finished work has several advantages—some practical, others aesthetic. From a practical viewpoint, proper care of a fabric hanging is most essential. Mounting protects the hanging from unraveling and snagging; it prevents buckling and creasing of glued pieces; and avoids pulling the stitched thread and yarns out of shape.

But the aesthetic advantages probably outweigh the practical, for very often the completed hanging needs a mount to accentuate the design. A mount gives emphasis, highlights the design, and unifies the composition so the component parts "hold together" as a unit.

There are still other ways in which the mount may affect the hanging. In most cases, it will separate the design from the wall, especially when framed. But, in some instances, the design may appear as part of the wall or as its extension. For example, very often a dowel rod mounting permits the fabric to cling to the wall, and a three-dimensional hanging may purposely be mounted to appear as an extended appendage of the wall.

Finding the right mount for the hanging is not always easy. What kind of mount does the design need? How can one determine if he has selected a mount that enhances his hanging? A good way to tell is to test one's reaction to what he sees. If he isn't sure, he should analyze his design and question the relationship between it and the mount. Which appears more important, the mount or the design? In summary, the mount should contribute to the hanging rather than overpower or dominate it.

Mounting on a paper background

Mounting the hanging can and should be uncomplicated. A paper background is an effective way to mount some kinds of work, for instance, small hangings made by children. For this simple mount, first prepare the edges of the hanging by cutting, fringing, or hemming the fabric. Place the design on a slightly larger contrasting paper (construction or tag-board), then staple a different color paper, larger than the first. If one desires a sturdier mount, he might staple or glue the fabric to a heavy colorful showcard board, allowing for a contrasting border.

Mat frames with and without backing are another way to mount hangings. With a sharp knife, these mounts can be cut in any size.

But for quick mounting, precut commercial mats are good. These, available in a variety of stock sizes, are more expensive than those you cut yourself but often their convenience outweighs the cost. And, with care, they are reusable.

Mounting on rods

Another popular and easy way to mount a hanging is to use a rod made of wood, brass, glass or plastic. These are available from the following sources: wood (dowel) rods in different diameters at hobby shops and lumber yards; brass rods from curtain shops and hardware stores; and glass rods at government surplus depots and scientific equipment suppliers.

If one wishes a substitute for the round rod, he might try a lattice strip. Like the dowel rod, it is available at lumber yards. But the most natural kind of rod is the tree branch. Its irregularity, when stripped of small twigs, adds a rustic interest to the top and bottom of almost any hanging.

Rods are used for mounting in different ways. Some hold the hanging at the top, others hold it at top and bottom, and still others add sturdiness to the hanging by becoming a decorative part of the design.

Branch support.   Student, Grade 4.

finishing a hanging

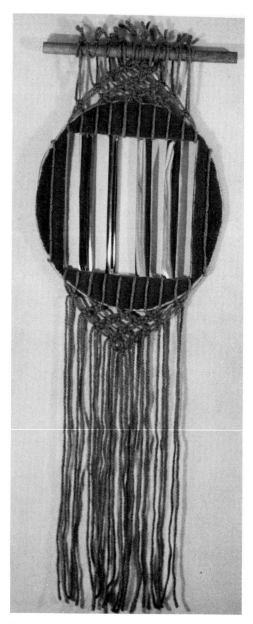

There are two basic methods of preparing a hanging to mount on a rod. Make a fairly wide hem for the rods at the top and bottom edge of the hanging, then insert the rods. Suspend the hanging by tying a cord near each end of the rod, or knot the ends and slip the cord near each end of the rod; or knot the ends and slip the cord through previously slit ends of the rod or lattice strip. Hem the top and bottom edges of the hanging. Stitch several additional pieces of fabric about three to five inches long and two or three inches wide. Then fold in half to form loops and stitch them to the edges (with one at each end and the others evenly spaced between them) at the top and bottom hem. The loops will form a decorative heading. Slip the rods through these to mount the hanging.

One may change the effect of the looped heading according to where he fastens the loops. They may be stitched along the front of each hem, stitched to the back of each hem and covered with a strip of material, or inserted between a front and its back lining.

Decorative headings have many possibilities. Two easy ways are the placing of loops on one edge only, or loops on both top and bottom.

Most unframed hangings need a weighted bottom to hold the fabric straight. Sometimes a rod is sufficient, otherwise try stitching metal weights to the back of the bottom hem. These weights, in different sizes, are available at hardware stores and sewing centers.

Mounting on rigid supports

Some hangings are more effectively mounted by simply stretching the fabric over a rigid background or frame. Such supports may include masonite, homosote, wallboard, and stretcher frames. To make fabrics taut, wrap them over the front and around the edges. Except for masonite which requires gluing or taping, attach the fabric to the support by stapling or tacking it to the back.

Artist, Lucia Suffel.

*Wool on linen with mylar strips. 15" x 36".
Artist, Patricia Malarcher.*

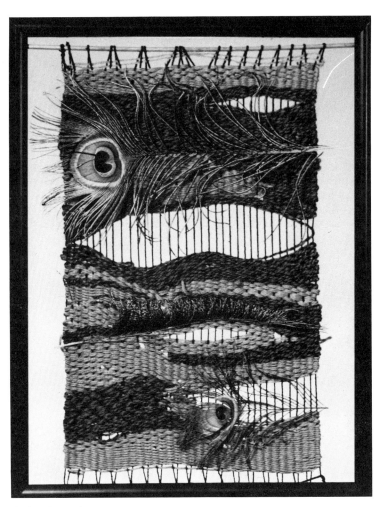

Artist, the author.

Stiff supports

Cardboard is a good base for a background, especially if stretching is required. For this kind of support, showcard and chip board are excellent. The fact that they will warp (flex a little and even buckle when left in a damp area) makes it necessary to store in a dry place.

For more permanent, rigid supports, experiment with masonite, insulation board, and canvas board. Each is available in varying sizes and, with a little persuasion, the cloth will stretch over the surface and one can tape or staple it around the edges on the back side.

Earth Fragments: Artist, Nancy Belfer.

Flexible supports

Most heavy fabrics make good background supports in themselves. Lined burlaps, monk's cloth, and linen hang especially well. But like most other fabrics, they are also effective when stretched over a stretcher frame.

Mural hangings

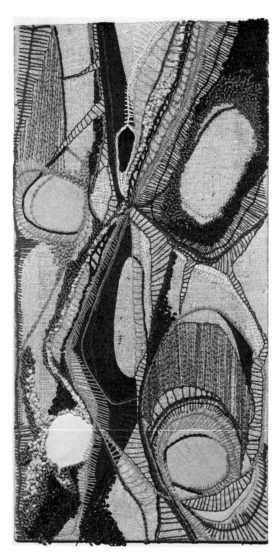

Appliqué and rug hooking.   Artist, Mary Grille Birkmeier.

Theme, Peter Rabbit.   Student, Grade 2.

Arranging shapes for different panels of mural. Students, Grade 2.

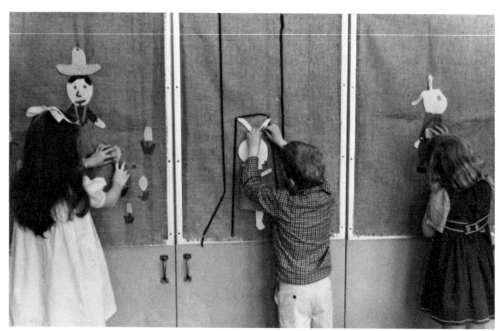

Journey Through 2 x Blue: executed for Svenska Handelsbanken, Sweden. Artist, Hans Krondahl, Sweden.

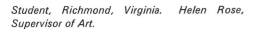

Student, Richmond, Virginia. Helen Rose, Supervisor of Art.

Thread and wire supports

Artist, Grete Schioler.

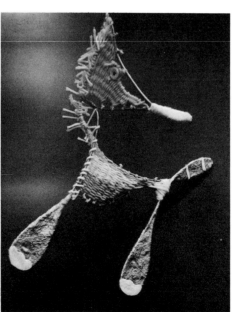

Dangling form: structure of reed, plaster embedded gauze and yarn.   Artist, Candace Milone.

Feather Pouch: natural linen. Artist, Susan Weitzman.

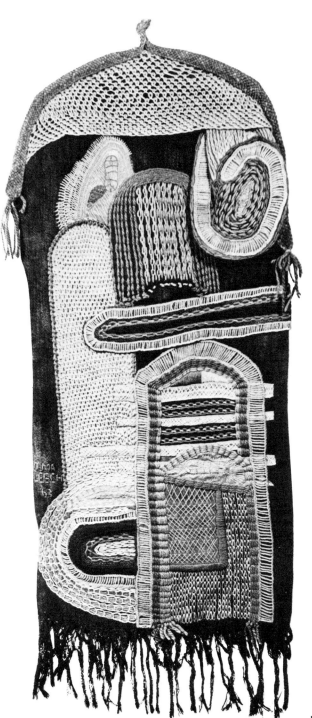

Joseph's Coat. Artist, Alma Lesch.

Assemblage.

Sarita Rainey at work on an assemblage of dried plant life, bells, stones, driftwood, and fabric.

Throughout this book are examples of many different works by children and adults—by beginners and professionals. Their work illustrates the innumerable ways designers see and think. Each had his own procedure for designing and executing his finished piece. Getting to know how different designers work and the environment in which they create suggests that we, too, find our own unique way of designing and making a wall hanging of fabric and thread.

artists at work

Henry Stahmer at work on a collage: colored advertisements torn and applied to fabric backing with glue and water. Stitchery worked over paper and fabric.

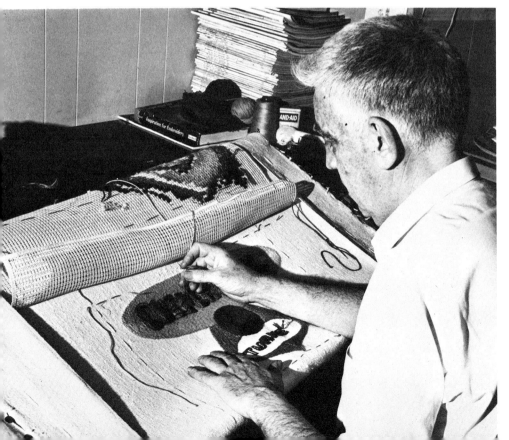

Henry Stahmer at work on a cross-stitch pattern: rug canvas is used as guide for cross-stitches, then removed when stitches are complete.

143

Marilyn Pappas.

C-For-7-Fred.   Artist, Marilyn Pappas.

Hans Krondahl of Sweden at work on appliqué.

Hans Krondahl checking completed design against a pre-planned pattern.

Jean A. Girdler gluing sequins on appliqué (far left).

Cartoon drawing (above). Artist, Frances Howell preparing the cartoon for needlepoint (right).

Everett Sturgeon.

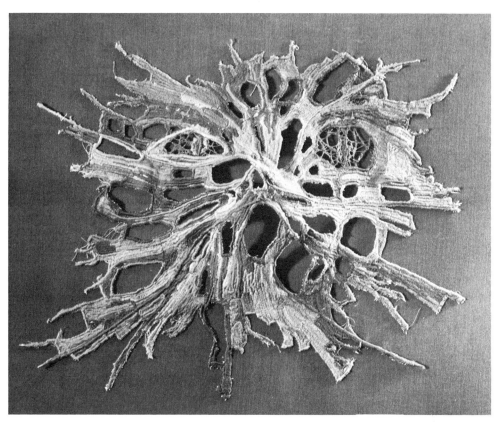

Wire soldered into rings and covered with zigzag machine stitching. Artist, Everett Sturgeon.

Wounded Forests. Artist, Ruth L. Ginsberg.

Soft Armour. Artist, Marie Tuicillo-Kelly.

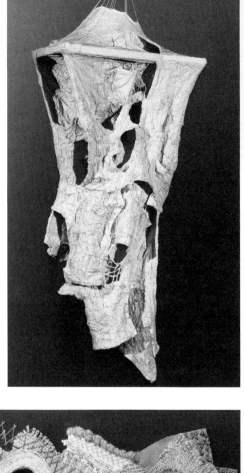

Serrano: burlap, wool, maguey and a variety of threads on a wool ground using stitchery, appliqué, and cut work. Artist, Evelyn Svec Ward.

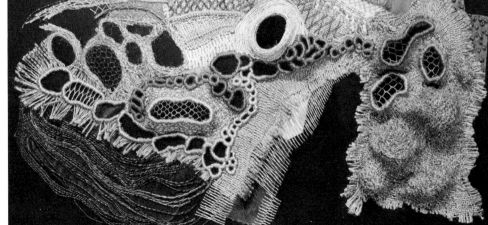

Snowflakes. Artist, Bianca Artom.

Artist, Kay Sekimachi.

Knotless netting combined with weaving. Artist, Evelyn Gulick. Photograph by Harry W. Crosby.

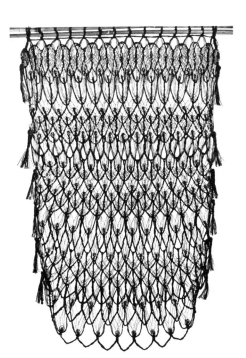

artists at work   149

appendix

**Guide for designing
wall hangings**

This guide suggests a variety of ways the designer may use to express his ideas.

Appliqué

Color — Accent with color.
Use different intensity of color.
Combine color.
Overlap parts of color.

Texture — Use smooth and rough fabrics; tightly and loosely woven cloth.
Make surface enrichments with string, yarn, non-fabric items (buttons, stones), different stitches, raw and frayed edgings.

Space — Cut different size shapes; vary the spacing between shapes; overlap shapes and lines.

Line — Make different width lines by pasting or stitching varying thicknesses of threads and yarns. Space strips at varying distances; overlap strips.
Outline shapes with fabric strips.
Accent design with string or yarn lines.
Use line to enclose a space.
Use line in different directions to make a pattern.

Shape — Vary the size or shapes.
Repeat some shape sizes.
Make each form similar in shape so they will appear related.

Designing backgrounds with threads and stitches

Color — Use contrasting thread and fabric.
Combine thick and thin threads to create tone.

Texture — Overlap line.
Space lines at varying distances.
Fill areas with line to make a solid pattern.

Space — Overlap lines.
Use lines that wander to create an overall pattern.
Use different kinds of lines: wavy, curved, jagged, circular.
Space lines at varying distances.

Line — Vary the thickness of line.
Vary the direction of line.

Shape — Enclose areas with line to make shapes.
Fill shapes with different stitches.

Canvas stitched hangings

Color — Use yarns of different shades and tones.

Texture — Expose parts of the canvas.
Use different kinds of yarns.
Make a solid background of flat stitches (such as the tent stitch) and apply other stitches, such as the chain, or ladder on top of them.

Space — Use different color wools to vary the appearance of shapes.
Outline some shapes.
Overlap shapes by letting shapes cut into one another.

Line	Make different width lines using a variety of stitches.
	Stitch over a determined number of canvas threads, then alter the number to vary the lines.
Shape	Make some shapes of solid stitching; expose parts of the canvas.
	Emphasize a shape by filling it with yarn and exposing the canvas surrounding it.
	Emphasize a shape by color intensity or hue.
	Fill some shapes with stitches in contrast with undecorated areas.

Quilting

Color	Appliqué colorful fabrics to the top quilt layer.
	Stitch through different thicknesses of interlinings to create high and low surfaces.
Texture	Create solid areas of stitching to make different patterns.
Space	Use different kinds of interlinings to vary the levels of relief surfaces.
Line	Use flowing lines over the total surface of the quilt.
	Enclose areas with tiny quilt stitching.
	Use line to emphasize one space or shape in contrast with other shapes.
Shape	Emphasize shape by stitching through an interlining that varies in thickness from one place to another.
	Use a double row of stitching to enclose a shape.

Decorative treatments

Color	Use contrasting threads and fabrics; combine shiny with dull materials.
	Accent with color.
Texture	Make surface decoration; bunch or pleat fabric; stitch on top of fabric; weave into fabric; use beads, clay, bone, seeds, glass, and thread items.
Space	Repeat the decoration using it at intervals throughout the design.
	Use the decoration to emphasize an area.
Line	Emphasize a shape with lines of stitches, beads, seeds, etc.
	Use decorative line to unify the design.
Shape	Weave under and over threads to make a surface pattern.
	Fill shapes with stitches.

Innovative combinations

Color	Overlap colors; repeat colors; experiment with contrasts and subtleties.
Texture	Strive for variety in texture using different kinds of fabrics and items such as sequins, leather, buttons, etc.
Space	Use fabrics on different plane levels.
	Suspend shapes of items.
Line	Use line to unify the design.
	Use line to define a shape.
Shape	Overlap shapes.
	Use open and closed shapes.
	Repeat shapes.
	Combine large and small shapes.

General supplies

Supplies for applique and stitchery are inexpensive and easily available. Here is a list to get one started:

Adhesives
New varieties of adhesives open many possibilities for the fabric and thread artist. Both solid pastes and liquid glues work well. Adhesives may include solid "school grade" paste, a rubber base adhesive (Tri-tex or Rubber Cement), white liquid glues that dry clear (Elmer's, P.V.A.-Polyvinyl Acetate), transparent glues that permit sewing through the glued area, and others such as Duco, Nu-Masters, and Amaco cements. Spray cements such as 3-M and Spra-ment adhesive adhere on contact. Any glue or paste should be applied sparingly to avoid discoloring the fabric.

Glues and pastes vary in their holding ability and their affinity to the material bonded. Solid adhesives and white emulsion glues are general bonding adhesives for lightweight materials. Heavy materials usually need more adhesive and longer drying periods. Some materials are more absorbent than others. Burlaps, synthetic cloths, cottons, linens, and woolens often require that the background supports have a pre-coating of polymer medium.

Needles
Consider the following three points when purchasing needles: What age level is going to use them? Large eye needles are best for children. The shaft is easy to manipulate and the big eye will thread easily. Plastic needles flex easily and the points are blunt.

Thread and Yarn
The design, needle, and background material determine the type of thread and yarn. Thread is purchased by number which denotes the size of the strand. Yarn is purchased by weight. Thin strands blend into finely woven fabric backgrounds; thicker strands suggest contrast. Heavyweight yarns require coarse background unless they are couched in place.

Fabric
A fabric may suggest an idea to the designer. Fabrics differ in texture (rough-smooth), composition (tight and loose weaves) and visual quality (opaque and translucent). Fabrics used for backgrounds will often determine the necessary kind of mounting. Flimsy materials will need a stretched mounting or a heavy lining to make them hang straight. See section on mounting.

Materials and Supplies

American Crewel Studios
Mrs. John Campbell
Box 553
Westfield, New Jersey 07091
	Fabrics:
	    Linen twills, Irish upholstery linen, Belgian linen, French single thread canvas, W. German canvas, others.
	Crewel Wools:
	    850 shades in stock.
	Needles

Barnes & Blake Box 240 Cooper Station, New York 10003	*Rug yarn, Persian and needlepoint wools, needlepoint and quickpoint canvas, linen.*
Boomfield Woolen Co. Bloomfield, Indiana 47424	*60" x 84" pieces.* *14 colors of pre-cut wool strips.*
Bon Bazar Ltd. 149 Waverly Place New York, New York 10014	*Burlap and felt in assorted colors.*

Ceramics and macramé with feathers. Artist, Shirley Marein.

Boutique Margot
26 W. 54
New York, New York 10019

Embroidery supplies, pure silks, gold and silver metallic threads.
Binca fabric for cross-stitch.

Colonial Needle
11 E. 31 St.
New York, New York 10016

Needles of various types.

D. Jay Products Inc.
P.O. Box 797
Newark, New Jersey 07101

Novelty threads and chenille stems.

House of Crewel
Chieftain Motel
Hanover, New Jersey 03755

Linens by the yard, crewel wool.

Light Leather Co. Ltd.
16 Soho Square
London W. 1. England

Leathers of different types.
Whole skins.

Lily Mills Co.
Shelby, North Carolina 28150

Cotton, wool, metallic, rayon yarns.

Needlecraft House
West Townsend, Massachusetts 01474

Crewel and tapestry yarn, carpet wools, embroidery hoops, needles, fabrics.

Richmond Brothers
Balfield Rd.
Dundee, Scotland

Glenshee fabrics.

Lisbeth Perrone
210 Riverside Drive
New York, New York 10025

Colorful linen yarns.

Needlecraft Shop
13561 Ventura Blvd.
Sherman Oaks, California 91403

Yarns:
Threads: Silk floss, twisted silk, stout silk, cotton, rayon, linen.
Frames, linens, foreign woolens, canvas, needles.

Joan Toggitt Ltd.
1170 Broadway
Rm. 406
New York, New York 10001

Springer and Marline threads or yarns.
Glenshee linens (for cross-stitch and counted thread stitchery) Assisi.
Evenweave linens. Imports from Scandinavia.

Watts & Co.
7 Tufton St.
Westminster, London SWI

Lurex fabrics, braids, cords.

Women's Education & Industrial Union
264 Boylston St.
Boston, Massachusetts 02116

Crewel and needlepoint supplies.
Blocking and mounting.

glossary

Appliqué—A two-dimensional approach of pasting one material on top of another. It includes the techniques of pasting, mono-rubbing, and stitching.

Assemblage—An extension of collage, which, along with paper, cardboard and cloth, includes such items as bark, buttons, and wood. These constructions might incorporate any of the design elements of shape, space, and rhythm. They are either two- or three-dimensional, often emerging as relief or freestanding sculptures.

Banner—A poster made of fabric. Basically, it presents one idea. The image is simple and bold, crystallizing the artist's idea in a concise visual statement.

Blackwork—A repeated counted thread pattern.

Collage—A design made by pasting or stitching different materials such as paper, cardboard, and cloth to a background.

Crewel—A thin, two-stranded worsted wool. It is a colorful material to use for a wall hanging.

Macramé—The art of knot tying.

Needlepoint—An embroidered mesh canvas. The size of mesh, the number of threads per inch whether single or double thread, determines the name of the embroidery: petit point (20 threads to the inch or smaller), needlepoint (14–18 threads to the inch), gros point (8–12 threads to the inch), bold stitch (5–7 threads to the inch).

Optical hangings—Designs that play on the eye with color, line, and shape. These moire effects (irregular, wavy or ripple patterns) keep the eye busy jumping from color to color or line to line, often emerging as distorted images.

Quilting—The technique of using three layers of material together—top, interlining, and bottom. The top and bottom may be of the same or different fabric, while cotton dacron batting, or flannel is good for the in-between layer. Stitching through the layers with tiny, running stitches holds the layers together and, at the same time, allows the unstitched parts to puff up.

Relief hangings—Projections at intermediate levels. Padded or stuffed areas that protrude in varying amounts from the background surface.

Reverse appliqué—A two-dimensional pattern made by placing one material under another, then cutting out areas of the top fabric to expose the underlying one.

Three-dimensional appliqué—Stuffed fabric forms that may be viewed from different sides.

Trapunto—A variation of quilting. A stuffed rather than a quilted design that gives a high relief. This technique requires the same materials as quilting but only two layers of fabric.

Cord quilting—A variation of quilting in which two parallel lines are stitched through a top and bottom fabric to form a channel through which a cord is inserted.

Hawaiian quilting—A quilt top composed of silhouette shapes similar to snowflake designs.

bibliography

King, Bucky *Creative Canvas Embroidery,* Hearthside Press, Inc., New York, 1963.

Sidney, Sylvia *Needlepoint Book,* Van Nostrand Reinhold Company, New York, 1968.

Enthoven, Jacqueline *The Stitches of Creative Embroidery,* Van Nostrand Reinhold Company, New York, 1964.

Butler, Anne *Embroidery Stitches: An Illustrated Guide,* Frederick A. Praeger, Inc., New York, 1968.

Harvey, Virginia *Macramé: The Art of Creative Knotting,* Van Nostrand Reinhold Company, New York, 1967.

Rainey, Sarita R. *Weaving Without A Loom,* Davis Publications, Inc., Worcester, Mass., 1966.

Horn, George F. *Art for Today's Schools,* Davis Publications, Inc., Worcester, Mass., 1967.

Hamlyn, Paul *Early Decorative Textiles,* The Hamlyn Publishing Group Limited, Hamlyn House, The Centre, Feltham, Middlesex, England, 1969.

Janis, Harriet and Blesh, Rudi *Collage Personalities, Concepts, Techniques,* Chilton Book Co., Philadelphia, Penn., 1967.

Runes & Schrickel *Encyclopedia of the Arts,* Philosophical Library, Inc.,. New York, 1946

Howard, Constance *Inspiration for Embroidery,* B. T. Batesford Ltd., Charles T. Branford Co., Boston, Mass., 1968.

Clarke, Leslie J. *The Craftsman in Textiles,* Frederick A. Praeger, Inc., New York, 1968.

Hall, Carrie A. & Kretsinger, Rose G. *The Romance of the Patchwork Quilt in America,* Bonanza Books, a division of Crown Publishers, Inc., New York, 1935.

Karasz, Mariska *Adventures in Stitches & More Adventures,* Funk & Wagnalls (a division of Reader's Digest Inc.), New York, 1959.

Anders, Nedda C. *Appliqué Old & New including Patchwork & Embroidery,* Hearthside Press, Inc., New York, 1967.

Beitler, Ethel Jane *Create with Yarn,* International Textbooks in Art Education, Philadelphia, Penn., 1964.

Guild, Vera P. *Creative Use of Stitches,* Davis Publications, Inc., Worcester, Mass., revised 1969.

Geddes & McNeill *Blackwork Embroidery,* Charles T. Branford Co., Boston, Mass., 1965.

VanDommelen, David B. *Decorative Wall Hangings, Art with Fabric,* Funk & Wagnalls Co., Inc., New York, 1962.

Seal skin appliqué by Eskimos. Cape Dorset, Circa 1951. Eskimo art collection of Dept. of Indian Affairs and Northern Development, Ottawa, Canada.

acknowledgments

I wish to express my gratitude and appreciation to Mr. Donald Wyckoff, Executive Vice President and National Director of American Crafts Council, for his interest in my work as artist and teacher and for the Foreword of this book. To those who provided special assistance, I wish to thank Lydia Bancroft, Professional Textile artist; Dr. Catherine Bates, Dean of Women, Georgetown University, Kentucky; Dr. Robert Cooke, Prof. of Art, Paterson State College, N.J.; Dr. Delbert Earisman, Prof. of English, Upsala College, N.J.; Dorothea Malcolm, Prof. of Art, Paterson State College, N.J.; M. Adam Salvo, Chairman H.S. Art Dept., Ridgefield, Conn.; Eugenia Claude, Coordinator Pupil Services, Montclair Public Schools; Vincent Popolizio; Chief, N.Y. State Art Supervisor, New York, Panagiota Darras, Boston, Mass.; May Melville, Montclair, N.J.; Rinita Hanfling, Contemporary Crafts Museum, N.Y.; Jean Mailey, Metropolitan Museum of Art, N.Y.; Edith Warsher, Denmark; Eleanor Nowlin, Vt.; Linda Loving, N.Y.; and Linda Kramer, N.Y.

To those who willingly accepted my suggestions, philosophy, and techniques in their teaching of art in the Montclair Public Schools, I wish to thank Eileen Scally, Louis Milone, Patricia Trotter, John Nace, Peter Langenbach, and Tom Hitmar.

For special services I express appreciation to The Metropolitan Museum of Art, The Museum of Modern Art, N.Y.; Shelburne Museum, Shelburne, Vt.; Contemporary Crafts Museum, N.Y.; Museum of Primitive Art, N.Y.; Brooklyn Museum of Art, N.Y.; The Cooper Hewitt Union Museum of the Smithsonian Institution, N.Y.; The Canadian Government, Ottawa; Embroiderers' Guild of Australia, London, England, and New York City.

S.R.R.